HEINEMANN
SHAKESPEARE

The Merchant of Venice

edited by Elizabeth Seely

with additional notes and activities by
Rick Lee and Stephanie Burgin

Series Editor: John Seely

In association with the RSA
Shakespeare in Schools Project

The RSA Shakespeare in Schools Project

The **Heinemann Shakespeare Series** has been developed in association with the **RSA Shakespeare in Schools Project**. Schools in the project have trialled teaching approaches to make Shakespeare accessible to students of all ages and ability levels.

John Seely has worked with schools in the project to develop the unique way of teaching Shakespeare to 11- to 16-year-olds found in **Heinemann Shakespeares**.

The project is a partnership between the RSA (Royal Society for the encouragement of Arts, Manufactures and Commerce), Leicestershire County Council and the Groby family of schools in Leicestershire. It is co-ordinated by the Knighton Fields Advisory Centre for Drama and Dance.

Heinemann Educational Publishers
Halley Court, Jordan Hill, Oxford OX2 8EJ
a division of Reed Educational & Professional Publishing Ltd
OXFORD   MELBOURNE   AUCKLAND
JOHANNESBURG   BLANTYRE   GABORONE
IBADAN   PORTSMOUTH (NH) USA   CHICAGO

Introduction, notes and activities © Elizabeth Seely, John Seely, Rick Lee 1994
Additional material by Stephanie Burgin

The text is based on the First Quarto of 1600, but modern scholars have been freely consulted and used.

Printed in the *Heinemann Shakespeare Plays* series 1994

08 07 06 05 04 03 02 01 00
16 15 14 13 12 11 10 9 8

A catalogue record for this book is availabl[e]
ISBN 0435 19205 1

Cover design Miller Craig and Cocking
Cover photograph from Donald Cooper

Produced by Green Door Design Ltd

Printed by Clays Ltd, St Ives plc

CONTENTS

Introduction: using this book

This is more than just an edition of *The Merchant of Venice* with a few notes. It is a complete guide to studying and enjoying the play.

It begins with an introduction to Shakespeare's theatre, and to the story and characters of the play.

At the end of the book there is guidance on studying the play:
- how to keep track of things as you work
- how to take part in a range of drama activities
- understanding Shakespeare's language
- exploring the main themes of the play
- studying the characters
- how to write about the play.

There are also questions and a glossary of specialist words you need when working on the play.

The central part of the book is, of course, the play itself. Here there are several different kinds of help on offer:

Summary: at the top of each double page there is a short summary of what happens on that page.

Grading: alongside the text is a shaded band to help you when working on the play:

1 This is very important text that you probably need to spend extra time on.

2 This is text that you need to read carefully.

3 This is text that you need to spend less time on.

Notes: difficult words, phrases and sentences are explained in simple English.

Extra summaries: for the 'white' text the notes are replaced by numbered summaries that give more detail than the ordinary page-by-page summaries.

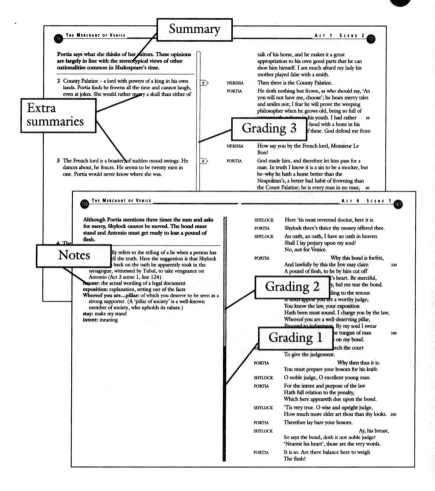

Summary

Extra summaries

Notes

Grading 3

Grading 2

Grading 1

THE MERCHANT OF VENICE

ACT 1 SCENE 2

Portia says what she thinks of her suitors. These opinions are largely in line with the stereotypical views of other nationalities common in Shakespeare's time.

2 County Palatine – a lord with powers of a king in his own lands. Portia finds he frowns all the time and cannot laugh, even at jokes. She would rather marry a skull than either of

3 The French lord is a boaster of sudden mood-swings. He dances about, he fences. He seems to be twenty men in one. Portia would never know where she was.

talk of his horse, and he makes it a great appropriation to his own good parts that he can shoe him himself. I am much afeard my lady his mother played false with a smith.

NERISSA   Then there is the County Palatine.

PORTIA   He doth nothing but frown, as who should say, 'An you will not have me, choose'; he hears merry tales and smiles not; I fear he will prove the weeping philosopher when he grows old, being so full of _____ in his youth. I had rather   50 _____ -head with a bone in his _____ f these. God defend me from

NERISSA   How say you by the French lord, Monsieur Le Bon?

PORTIA   God made him, and therefore let him pass for a man. In truth I know it is a sin to be a mocker, but he–why he hath a horse better than the Neapolitan's, a better bad habit of frowning than the Count Palatine; he is every man in no man;   60

THE MERCHANT OF VENICE

ACT 4 SCENE 1

Although Portia mentions three times the sum and asks for mercy, Shylock cannot be moved. The bond must stand and Antonio must get ready to lose a pound of flesh.

4 The _____ lly refers to the telling of a lie when a person has _____ ll the truth. Here the suggestion is that Shylock _____ back on the oath he apparently took in the synagogue, witnessed by Tubal, to take vengeance on Antonio (Act 3 scene 1, line 124).
tenour: the actual wording of a legal document
exposition: explanation, setting out of the facts
Whereof you are...pillar: of which you deserve to be seen as a strong supporter. (A 'pillar of society' is a well-known member of society, who upholds its values.)
stay: make my stand
intent: meaning

SHYLOCK   Here 'tis most reverend doctor, here it is.

PORTIA   Shylock there's thrice thy money offered thee.

SHYLOCK   An oath, an oath, I have an oath in heaven. Shall I lay perjury upon my soul? No, not for Venice.

PORTIA   Why this bond is forfeit, And lawfully by this the Jew may claim   230 A pound of flesh, to be by him cut off _____ 's heart. Be merciful, _____ y, bid me tear the bond. _____ ding to the tenour. It doth appear you are a worthy judge; You know the law, your exposition Hath been most sound. I charge you by the law, Whereof you are a well-deserving pillar, Proceed to judgement. By my soul I swear _____ he tongue of man   240 _____ on my bond. _____ ech the court To give the judgement.

PORTIA   Why then thus it is: You must prepare your bosom for his knife.

SHYLOCK   O noble judge, O excellent young man.

PORTIA   For the intent and purpose of the law Hath full relation to the penalty, Which here appeareth due upon the bond.

SHYLOCK   'Tis very true. O wise and upright judge, How much more elder art thou than thy looks.   250

PORTIA   Therefore lay bare your bosom.

SHYLOCK   Ay, his breast, So says the bond, doth it not noble judge? 'Nearest his heart', those are the very words.

PORTIA   It is so. Are there balance here to weigh The flesh?

Activities

After every few scenes there is a section containing things to do, helping you focus on the scenes you have just read:
- questions to make sure you have understood the story
- discussion points about the themes and characters of the play
- drama activities
- character work
- close study to help you understand the language of the play
- writing activities.

Shakespeare's theatre

Heavens the roof above the stage, supported by pillars. Characters could be lowered to the stage during the play

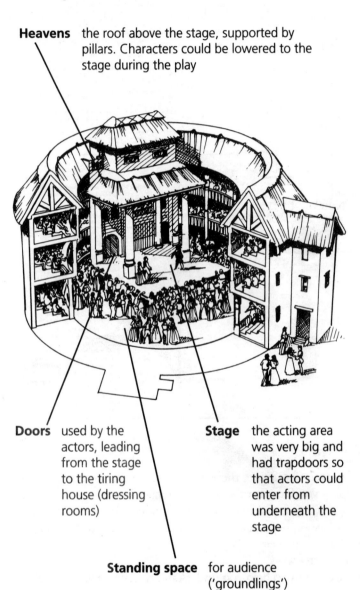

Doors used by the actors, leading from the stage to the tiring house (dressing rooms)

Stage the acting area was very big and had trapdoors so that actors could enter from underneath the stage

Standing space for audience ('groundlings')

Below is a scene from *The Merchant of Venice* showing both the inner stage and the gallery in use for the action of the play.

When you have studied the play, you should be able to work out exactly which moment in the play this shows.

Gallery used for action on an upper level (or, if not, for musicians)

Inner stage curtained area that could be opened up to show a new scene

Going to the theatre in Shakespeare's day

Theatre-going was very popular in Elizabethan London, but it was very different from going to a play today. It was like a cross between going to a football match and going to the theatre. The playhouses were open air and the lack of artificial lighting meant that plays were performed in daylight, normally in the afternoon.

Places were not reserved, so people had to arrive in plenty of time – often more than an hour before the play was due to start. They paid a penny to get into the playhouse, so it was not cheap, since a penny was about one twelfth of a day's wages for a skilled workman. Your penny let you into the large open yard surrounding the stage. The audience here had to stand, looking up at the actors (the stage was 1.5–1.8 metres above the ground). If people wanted a seat, then they had to pay another penny or twopence. This gave admission to the tiers of seating surrounding the yard, and also meant that you had a roof over your head, in case it started to rain. People with even more money could pay to have a seat in an enclosed room. So people of all incomes and social classes attended the theatre and paid for the kind of accommodation they wanted.

While the audience was waiting for the play to begin, people had time to meet friends, talk, eat and drink – in fact they used to continue to enjoy themselves in this way while the play was being performed. But Elizabethan audiences were knowledgeable and enthusiastic. Watching a play was an exciting experience; although the stage was very big, the theatre was quite small, so no-one was far from the actors. When an actor had a soliloquy (solo speech) he could come right into the middle of the audience and speak his thoughts in a natural, personal way. At the other extreme, the large stage and the three different levels meant that whole battles could be enacted, complete with cannon fire, thunder and lightning and loud military music.

There was no painted stage scenery, so that the audience had to use their imagination to picture the location of each scene, but Shakespeare always gave plenty of word clues in the characters' speeches of when and where a scene took place. The lack of scenery to move about also meant that scene could follow scene without any break. On the other hand, the theatre companies spared no expense on costumes and furniture and other properties; plays also had live music performed by players placed either in the auditorium close to the stage, or in the gallery above it, if that was not to be used in the play.

Altogether Londoners especially must have considered that going to the theatre was an exciting and important part of their lives; it is believed that up to a fifth of them went to the theatre regularly. Shakespeare and the company in which he became a shareholder, the Lord Chamberlain's Men, worked hard and became wealthy men.

The characters of the play

Prince of Morocco

Portia

Prince of Arragon

Nerissa

Tubal

Shylock

Jessica

Launcelot Gobbo

Old Gobbo

Gratiano

Salerio

Solanio

Lorenzo

Bassanio

Antonio

The story of the play

Antonio, a rich merchant, is, without any obvious reason, in a depressed state. His friends suggest he is worried about his merchant ships, or that he is in love. He dismisses both suggestions.

Antonio has in the past lent money to his friend Bassanio. This time Bassanio wants to set himself up to try for the hand in marriage of Portia, a wealthy and beautiful heiress. To finance this, Antonio now has to borrow money, as all his resources are at present in his ships, trading to distant countries.

At Belmont, her newly-inherited estate about twenty miles from Venice, Portia feels frustrated by the terms of her father's will. He has laid down that everyone who hopes to marry her must choose between a casket of gold, silver or lead. Portia will have to accept as her husband the man who demonstrates sound values by making the 'correct' choice. Nerissa, Portia's companion, tries to persuade her that it is all for the best. All the suitors must also take an oath never to marry if they fail in this contest. Half a dozen totally unsuitable young men decide to leave without taking their chance. The next candidate is the Prince of Morocco.

Back in Venice, Bassanio approaches Shylock, a wealthy Jew, who lends money in return for interest, which at that time Christians were not allowed to do. Shylock and Antonio are already enemies. Each of them hates what the other stands for. Antonio admits that he has spat on Shylock and called him names. He has also rescued people heavily in debt to Shylock. This affects Shylock's livelihood. Shylock agrees to lend 3,000 ducats on Antonio's bond. He tries to persuade Antonio that usury is sanctioned in the Bible. On this occasion, instead of taking a percentage of the loan as interest, Shylock offers a 'joke' bond – the forfeit of a pound of Antonio's flesh if the loan is not repaid in three months. Antonio agrees to this against Bassanio's advice.

Launcelot Gobbo, currently Shylock's servant, wants to leave Shylock's service, but is having a battle with his conscience. He has some fun at the expense of his elderly father and then together they ask Bassanio to take Launcelot on as his servant. Bassanio agrees. Shylock's daughter, Jessica, also plans to run away from him. She uses Launcelot to take messages to her lover, Lorenzo, with whom she is going to elope.

Before Bassanio leaves for Belmont with his rather unruly friend Gratiano, he invites all his friends to dinner. Shylock is to be there also and this gives Lorenzo and Jessica their chance. She dresses as a page and, having taken money and jewels from her father, she leaves his house for ever. Before the party can take place, however, Bassanio and Gratiano must take advantage of the weather and sail for Belmont.

Meanwhile, at Belmont, the Prince of Morocco has chosen the golden casket, thus failed the test, and left. The Prince of Arragon has chosen silver and he too has gone away, disappointed.

Shylock seems distressed almost to madness by the loss at the same time of his daughter, a considerable amount of money and jewellery of real and sentimental value. He learns of Lorenzo's and Jessica's spending spree and is then a little comforted by persistent rumours of shipwreck affecting Antonio's cargoes. He is now looking for vengeance.

Portia and Bassanio are instantly attracted to each other. Unlike the two princes, he sees all the virtues of plain lead, and makes the right choice. They are both ecstatically happy and Portia gives Bassanio her ring, making him promise never to part with it. Gratiano and Nerissa have also fallen in love and she too gives him her ring, on the same terms.

Lorenzo and Jessica arrive, bringing a letter from Antonio. All his ships have sunk and his forfeit is being claimed by Shylock. Portia, realizing Bassanio's distress, arranges a speedy wedding for the two couples and sends the two men back to Venice with an offer of several times the original loan. Lorenzo and Jessica stay to look after the house as Portia pretends that she and Nerissa are going to a religious retreat to pray for their husbands. In fact, they are going to Venice, supplied with lawyers' robes and helpful legal opinion from one of Portia's cousins, Bellario.

Antonio has been allowed to visit Shylock from gaol to try to persuade him to be lenient. Shylock, however, is bent on revenge. In court Antonio makes it clear he is resigned to his fate. He knows the law cannot, in fact must not, be altered for one man's convenience. After appealing in vain to Shylock for mercy, Portia confirms the law, to Shylock's delight.

He has all the grisly apparatus prepared, the knife and the scales, and Antonio is stripped and ready when Portia points out that no blood must be spilt or Shylock must die. Further, because he has tried to kill a Venetian citizen, half his goods go to his intended victim and half to the state. Also, only the Duke can spare his life. Showing the mercy which Shylock would not, the Duke spares Shylock's life and at Antonio's request he can keep half his wealth as long as the other half may go to Lorenzo and Jessica and the rest to them on his death. Shylock must also become a Christian. He is a broken man.

As the lawyer and clerk, the only gifts Portia and Nerissa will accept for their services from Antonio and Bassanio are the rings they gave their husbands. These are parted with reluctantly.

Arriving back at a serene and beautiful Belmont, Portia and Nerissa soon confront their 'husbands' betrayal' and suggest the missing rings were given to women. They clear up the misunderstandings. Lorenzo and Jessica are delighted to learn of their future fortune and Antonio discovers that three of his ships have come safely to harbour after all.

Background

Date of the play

Scholars have suggested that Shakespeare wrote *The Merchant of Venice* some time between the late summer of 1596 and 1598. The evidence for this depends on detective work.

After several setbacks in the war against Spain, the Earl of Essex planned a naval expedition to attack and capture the Spanish port of Cadiz. Ninety-three English and 18 Dutch ships sailed from Plymouth in June 1596. Three weeks later they made a surprise attack on Cadiz, which was undefended. The Spaniards were burning their own ships to prevent their capture, but the English seized the *San Matias* and *San Andres* and took them back to England.

The *San Andres*, a splendid ship, was renamed the *Andrew*. The ship made several well-publicized voyages but it does not seem likely that it would have become generally recognized as the symbol of a rich trading ship until the following year. This dating is based on line 27 in Act 1 scene 1: '*And see my wealthy Andrew docked in sand.*'

So the likelihood is that *The Merchant of Venice* went into the repertory of the Lord Chamberlain's Men (Shakespeare's theatre company) in the 1597 season. The first performance of the play is not likely to have been later than 1598 because that is the date given for its appearance in a register of published plays. Plays were not usually printed until after their first successful season on the stage.

Plot and characters

Shakespeare is believed to have taken the story of this play from an Italian short story of the late fourteenth century. The scene is set in Venice and at Belmont. The Lady of Belmont sets a different task for her suitors, but the other elements are very similar to Shakespeare's play. The young man who eventually wins the lady has lost valuable ships before, his benefactor (in the short story his godfather) has to pledge a pound of flesh to a Jewish moneylender. When the bond falls due, the lady offers ten times the pledge. When the Jew refuses, she comes to court in disguise, as Portia does, and wins. The story of the rings is there, too.

Shakespeare adds the story of the caskets, gives his Jew a daughter and leaves Antonio unmarried.

There is also a suggestion that Shakespeare was competing with a very popular play *The Jew of Malta* written in 1589 by Christopher Marlowe. This play treats the Jew, called Barabas, as a thoroughly evil villain, a wicked ogre. Shakespeare is not entirely free from the idea that usurer = Jew = evil, but he does allow us to see Shylock as a human being who has himself been wronged.

Jews in England

In theory only Jews who had converted to Christianity were allowed to live in England in Shakespeare's day. Jews who practised their own religion were banned from England in 1290 and only readmitted by Oliver Cromwell in the seventeenth century.

The year after his early death in 1593, Marlowe's play became even more popular. In 1594 Queen Elizabeth I's doctor was executed for high treason.

- He was a Portuguese Jew, Dr Roderigo Lopez, who had converted to Christianity thirty-five years previously and was a fashionable society doctor in London.
- The charge against him was that he had plotted to poison Queen Elizabeth. This was doubted then and is now, but there was much public prejudice against him. He was a foreigner and a Jew.
- What does seem clear is that he was a spy for the English in their dealings with Spain and Portugal, and almost certainly a double-agent – a dangerous trade. He was hanged, drawn and quartered, and people flocked to Marlowe's play.

Antisemitism

In his book *Antisemitism: The Longest Hatred* Robert S. Wistrich traces the origins of antisemitism to pagan times. Simplified, he believes the main elements are:

- When, in the third century BC, some Jews moved out of the Holy Land to Greece and Rome, they did not intermingle with non-Jews (Gentiles); they kept to their belief in one God; they preserved their laws on what food they were allowed to eat; they maintained their separate lifestyle and above all their pride in being God's chosen people.
- The resentment this pattern of behaviour caused soon became mixed with myth and superstition, including the accusation of ritual murder. Historians started to write about this as though it were fact. Because Jews kept to themselves they were accused of being unpatriotic, and 'haters of mankind'.
- The other side of this in the first century AD was the Jews' insistence that they were superior to the 'heathen' around them. They attempted to convert people to the Jewish religion and were successful. Thus at the beginning of the Christian era in the Roman Empire there were some ten million Jews (10–12 per cent of the total population). Of course this success also caused resentment, as did their success in business and in learning, which brought them wealth, power and privilege.
- Jesus was born, lived and died as a Jew in first-century Roman Palestine. So did his parents and his disciples. So early Christianity was born out of Judaism.
- Jesus was crucified by the occupying power – Rome – as a troublesome Jewish agitator. However, Wistrich claims, the story of the death of Jesus as told in the New Testament shifts responsibility for his crucifixion from the Romans to the Jews. This, the killing of the son of God, is the most frequently given 'reason' today for hatred of the Jews.

Prejudice

Throughout the centuries Jews have been subjected to massacres, and to forced conversion to Christianity. They have been outlawed from several European countries. They have been made to live in a ghetto – a part of the town reserved for them.

- It is impossible to give a reason for prejudice because there is no 'reason' for it. There is no 'reason' for bullying or for wars of religion. The sad fact is that people are easily frightened and feel threatened by what seems strange to them and by what they can't be bothered to try to understand. This includes, of course, different skin colour, different language, different culture, different habits, different beliefs – anything seen as 'different' in fact.

- People in power have often found this very useful. Hitler, for instance, with continuous propaganda for many years, managed to persuade his public that most of their troubles would be solved if they could get rid of the Jews.

- His task was made easier by the fact that he could invent 'an international conspiracy' as part of his racist plan, because most countries in the world today have Jews as their citizens. For his extermination programme to succeed, however, he needed to make the victims seem 'non-human'. Tolerance disappears as soon as you make people forget that everyone, whatever their race, religion or colour, feels just the same if hurt, either by words, or by physical violence.

THE MERCHANT
OF VENICE

CHARACTERS

THE DUKE OF VENICE

THE PRINCE OF MOROCCO ⎱ suitors to Portia
THE PRINCE OF ARRAGON ⎰

ANTONIO, a Merchant of Venice

BASSANIO, his friend, suitor to Portia

SOLANIO ⎱
SALERIO ⎰ friends to Antonio and Bassanio
GRATIANO

LORENZO, in love with Jessica

SHYLOCK, a rich Jew

TUBAL, a Jew, his friend

LAUNCELOT GOBBO, a clown, servant to Shylock

OLD GOBBO, father to Launcelot

LEONARDO, servant to Bassanio

BALTHASAR ⎱ servants to Portia
STEPHANO ⎰

PORTIA, an heiress

NERISSA, her waiting-woman

JESSICA, daughter to Shylock

Magnificoes of Venice, Officers of the Court of Justice, Gaoler,
Musicians, Servants, and other Attendants

SCENE *Venice, and Portia's house at Belmont*

Antonio, a merchant, tells his friends he feels sad without knowing why. They say he is concerned about his ships and cargoes.

sooth: truth
whereof it is born: what causes it
I am to learn: I don't yet know
such a want-wit...myself: it puts me in such a senseless state of sadness that I scarcely know who or what I am
argosies: large merchant ships
portly sail: sails swollen by the wind
signiors and rich burghers: gentlemen and rich citizens (well-fed and so 'portly')
pageants: carnival floats
overpeer: tower above and look down on
petty traffickers: small merchant ships
curtsy: bob about
do them reverence: bow to them
woven wings: sails
venture: a business investment with the chance of making more money but the risk of losing the money put in
The better part: most
still: all the time
Plucking the grass: picking a blade of grass and holding it up to see which way the wind is blowing
roads: sheltered waters near the shore where ships can anchor safely.
wind: breath
broth: soup
ague: fever; shivering fit from fever or fear
flats: mud flats; invisible under water and so dangerous to ships

Act one

Scene

Venice

Enter ANTONIO, SALERIO, *and* SOLANIO

ANTONIO   In sooth I know not why I am so sad.
          It wearies me, you say it wearies you;
          But how I caught it, found it, or came by it,
          What stuff 'tis made of, whereof it is born,
          I am to learn.
          And such a want-wit sadness makes of me,
          That I have much ado to know myself.

SALERIO   Your mind is tossing on the ocean,
          There, where your argosies with portly sail,
          Like signiors and rich burghers on the flood,   10
          Or as it were the pageants of the sea,
          Do overpeer the petty traffickers
          That curtsy to them, do them reverence,
          As they fly by them with their woven wings.

SOLANIO   Believe me, sir, had I such venture forth,
          The better part of my affections would
          Be with my hopes abroad. I should be still
          Plucking the grass to know where sits the wind,
          Peering in maps for ports and piers and roads;
          And every object that might make me fear   20
          Misfortune to my ventures, out of doubt
          Would make me sad.

SALERIO   My wind, cooling my broth,
          Would blow me to an ague when I thought
          What harm a wind too great might do at sea.
          I should not see the sandy hour-glass run,
          But I should think of shallows and of flats,

Antonio assures them he has no need to worry about his ships. He rejects the suggestion that he might be in love.

Andrew: usually taken to refer to a real Spanish ship, the *San Andres*, which the English captured at Cadiz in 1596 and took into their fleet
Vailing: lowering, letting down
high-top: topsail
burial: grave
Should I go: If I were to go
edifice: building
bethink me: be reminded of
straight: immediately
gentle: gallant
stream: ocean
Enrobe: dress
but even now worth this: a moment ago so valuable
Shall I...sad?: Is it possible that I should have these thoughts without realizing I would feel sad if such things actually happened?
But tell not me: Don't bother to tell me
ventures: enterprises
bottom: ship
Upon: at risk on
Fie, fie!: an exclamation of dismay or disgust

1 >

1 Solanio suggests that if there really is no reason for Antonio's sadness, he might just as well be cheerful.

2 >

2 He concludes that there are people who are cheerful and people who are miserable, whatever the circumstances, just as the Roman god Janus (really just the god of exits and entrances) was (wrongly) supposed to have a different expression for each of his two heads.

3 Bassanio, Lorenzo and Gratiano arrive.

3 >

And see my wealthy Andrew docked in sand,
Vailing her high-top lower than her ribs
To kiss her burial. Should I go to church
And see the holy edifice of stone,   30
And not bethink me straight of dangerous rocks,
Which touching but my gentle vessel's side
Would scatter all her spices on the stream,
Enrobe the roaring waters with my silks,
And, in a word, but even now worth this,
And now worth nothing? Shall I have the thought
To think on this, and shall I lack the thought
That such a thing bechanced would make me sad?
But tell not me, I know Antonio
Is sad to think upon his merchandise.   40

ANTONIO   Believe me no, I thank my fortune for it,
My ventures are not in one bottom trusted,
Nor to one place; nor is my whole estate
Upon the fortune of this present year.
Therefore my merchandise makes me not sad.

SALERIO   Why then you are in love.

ANTONIO   Fie, fie!

SOLANIO   Not in love neither: then let us say you are sad
Because you are not merry; and 'twere as easy
For you to laugh and leap and say you are merry
Because you are not sad. Now by two-headed
     Janus,   50
Nature hath framed strange fellows in her time:
Some that will evermore peep through their eyes
And laugh like parrots at a bagpiper;
And other of such vinegar aspect
That they'll not show their teeth in way of smile
Though Nestor swear the jest be laughable.

Enter BASSANIO, LORENZO, *and* GRATIANO

Here comes Bassanio your most noble kinsman,
Gratiano, and Lorenzo. Fare ye well,

When Salerio and Solanio have left, Gratiano comments on Antonio's unhappy state, and starts to give Antonio advice.

---

4 Salerio and Solanio leave after greeting the newcomers.

5 Gratiano comments that Antonio does not look well. Antonio claims his own part in life is a sad one. The talkative Gratiano prefers the idea of playing the fool.

6 Gratiano starts to give advice. There are men, he says, who try to gain people's good opinion by remaining silent, and so appear full of wisdom, whereas if they spoke, people would know them for fools. Antonio should not be like this.

4 >

5 >

6 >

We leave you now with better company.

SALERIO   I would have stayed till I had made you merry,   60
If worthier friends had not prevented me.

ANTONIO   Your worth is very dear in my regard.
I take it your own business calls on you,
And you embrace th'occasion to depart.

SALERIO   Good morrow my good lords.

BASSANIO   Good signiors both, when shall we laugh? Say, when?
You grow exceeding strange. Must it be so?

SALERIO   We'll make our leisures to attend on yours.
                       [*Exeunt Salerio and Solanio*

LORENZO   My Lord Bassanio, since you have found Antonio,
We two will leave you, but at dinner-time   70
I pray you have in mind where we must meet.

BASSANIO   I will not fail you.

GRATIANO   You look not well Signior Antonio,
You have too much respect upon the world.
They lose it that do buy it with much care;
Believe me you are marvellously changed.

ANTONIO   I hold the world but as the world, Gratiano,
A stage where every man must play a part,
And mine a sad one.

GRATIANO   Let me play the fool;
With mirth and laughter let old wrinkles
   come,   80
And let my liver rather heat with wine
Than my heart cool with mortifying groans.
Why should a man whose blood is warm within,
Sit like his grandsire cut in alabaster?
Sleep when he wakes? And creep into the jaundice
By being peevish? I tell thee what Antonio–
I love thee, and it is my love that speaks–
There are a sort of men whose visages
Do cream and mantle like a standing pond,
And do a wilful stillness entertain,   90

Gratiano continues to warn Antonio not to adopt a false pose of silence, in order to be regarded as a wise man. Antonio and Bassanio are finally left alone. Bassanio has promised to reveal to Antonio the name of the lady he wishes to visit.

7 Lorenzo makes it clear Gratiano is far too talkative. They both leave.

7 >

reasons: explanations

pilgrimage: this word is usually reserved for a journey to places of great importance to world religions, or to the shrine of a saint

How much...continuance: how much money I have spent displaying a higher standard of living than my small income could continue to support.

With purpose to be dressed in an opinion
Of wisdom, gravity, profound conceit,
As who should say, 'I am Sir Oracle,
And when I ope my lips let no dog bark'.
O my Antonio, I do know of these
That therefore only are reputed wise
For saying nothing; when I am very sure
If they should speak, would almost damn those ears,
Which hearing them would call their brothers fools.
I'll tell thee more of this another time.   100
But fish not with this melancholy bait
For this fool gudgeon, this opinion.
Come good Lorenzo. Fare ye well awhile,
I'll end my exhortation after dinner.

LORENZO   Well, we will leave you then till dinner-time.
I must be one of these same dumb wise men,
For Gratiano never lets me speak.

GRATIANO   Well, keep me company but two years moe,
Thou shalt not know the sound of thine own tongue.

ANTONIO   Fare you well: I'll grow a talker for this gear.   110

GRATIANO   Thanks i'faith, for silence is only commendable
In a neat's tongue dried, and a maid not vendible.
                              [*Exeunt Gratiano and Lorenzo*

ANTONIO   Is that anything now?

BASSANIO   Gratiano speaks an infinite deal of nothing, more
than any man in all Venice. His reasons are as two
grains of wheat hid in two bushels of chaff: you
shall seek all day ere you find them, and when you
have them, they are not worth the search.

ANTONIO   Well, tell me now what lady is the same
To whom you swore a secret pilgrimage,   120
That you today promised to tell me of?

BASSANIO   'Tis not unknown to you Antonio,
How much I have disabled mine estate,
By something showing a more swelling port

Bassanio acknowleges that he has been living above his income. He owes most to Antonio, but asks him to lend still more in the hope of getting at least some of it back. Antonio promises all he has.

Nor do I...rate: Neither am I complaining now at having to cut down on my high spending

care: concern

come fairly off: discharge honourably

my time: my youth

something too prodigal: rather too wasteful

gaged: tangled

And from...warranty: because I know you love me, I am able

And...honour: If it (the plan) is honourable as you yourself always are

extremest means: all my wealth

Lie...occasions: are all available to meet your needs

shaft: arrow

fellow of the selfsame flight: another, identical arrow. (The '*flight*' is the particular pattern of feathers on the arrow that determines how the arrow will fly.)

advised: careful

urge: insist on

self: same

or...or: either...or

latter hazard: second amount of money risked

rest: remain

herein...circumstance: by speaking like this, you are wasting time appealing to my affection in such a roundabout way

making...uttermost: doubting I would do the very most I could

prest unto it: ready to do it, committed to it

Than my faint means would grant continuance;
Nor do I now make moan to be abridged
From such a noble rate, but my chief care
Is to come fairly off from the great debts
Wherein my time, something too prodigal,
Hath left me gaged. To you Antonio   130
I owe the most in money and in love,
And from your love I have a warranty
To unburden all my plots and purposes
How to get clear of all the debts I owe.

ANTONIO   I pray you good Bassanio let me know it,
And if it stand as you yourself still do,
Within the eye of honour, be assured
My purse, my person, my extremest means
Lie all unlocked to your occasions.

BASSANIO   In my school days, when I had lost one shaft,   140
I shot his fellow of the selfsame flight
The selfsame way, with more advised watch
To find the other forth, and by adventuring both
I oft found both. I urge this childhood proof
Because what follows is pure innocence.
I owe you much, and like a wilful youth,
That which I owe is lost, but if you please
To shoot another arrow that self way
Which you did shoot the first, I do not doubt,
As I will watch the aim, or to find both,   150
Or bring your latter hazard back again,
And thankfully rest debtor for the first.

ANTONIO   You know me well, and herein spend but time
To wind about my love with circumstance;
And out of doubt you do me now more wrong
In making question of my uttermost
Than if you had made waste of all I have.
Then do but say to me what I should do
That in your knowledge may by me be done,
And I am prest unto it. Therefore speak.   160

Bassanio now needs money to equip himself to go to
Belmont as a suitor for Portia, a rich and beautiful heiress,
whom many men wish to marry. Antonio promises him
the money – if he is able to borrow it.

richly left: a rich heiress
fair: beautiful and also with a fair complexion
fairer than that word: even more than that word implies
virtues: qualities
nothing undervalued: not inferior in value. Portia was the
  name of the daughter of Cato, a Roman statesman, general,
  and opponent of Caesar. Married to Brutus, one of the
  conspirators who murdered Caesar, she was highly thought
  of for her loyalty and love for her husband, and her
  intelligence and learning.
Renowned: famous
golden fleece/Colchos/Jason: In Greek myth Jason gathered
  together a crew for the ship *Argos* in which they sailed
  through dangerous seas to fetch the golden fleece from
  Colchis. It was guarded by a fierce dragon but Medea, the
  daughter of the King of Colchis, helped them to win it and
  escape with it and her. However, she had used witchcraft
  and the story ended in tragedy.
seat: estate
Colchos' strand: the country of Colchis
presages me such thrift: foretells such success for me
commodity: goods
present sum: instant cash
racked: stretched (as on the rack, an instrument of torture)
To...Portia: To fit you out to visit the beautiful Portia at
  Belmont
presently: straightaway
of my...sake: on my credit or out of regard for me

in the same abundance as: as many as

BASSANIO	In Belmont is a lady richly left,
	And she is fair, and fairer than that word,
	Of wondrous virtues–sometimes from her eyes
	I did receive fair speechless messages.
	Her name is Portia, nothing undervalued
	To Cato's daughter, Brutus' Portia.
	Nor is the wide world ignorant of her worth,
	For the four winds blow in from every coast
	Renowned suitors, and her sunny locks
	Hang on her temples like a golden fleece, 170
	Which makes her seat of Belmont Colchos' strand,
	And many Jasons come in quest of her.
	O my Antonio, had I but the means
	To hold a rival place with one of them,
	I have a mind presages me such thrift,
	That I should questionless be fortunate.

ANTONIO	Thou know'st that all my fortunes are at sea,
	Neither have I money nor commodity
	To raise a present sum. Therefore go forth;
	Try what my credit can in Venice do, 180
	That shall be racked even to the uttermost
	To furnish thee to Belmont to fair Portia.
	Go presently inquire, and so will I,
	Where money is, and I no question make
	To have it of my trust, or for my sake.

[Exeunt

Scene 2

Belmont

Enter PORTIA *and* NERISSA

| PORTIA | By my troth Nerissa, my little body is aweary of this great world. |

| NERISSA | You would be, sweet madam, if your miseries were in the same abundance as your good fortunes are; |

Portia's father has decreed that she must marry the man who makes the correct choice between three caskets, of gold, silver and lead. Portia finds this hard to take. Nerissa tries to reassure her. They start to discuss the suitors so far.

---

for aught I see: as far as I can see
surfeit: are overfilled
mean: small
mean: middle area
superfluity...hairs: excess soon makes people seem old
competency: moderation
sentences: wise sayings and court judgements
pronounced: expressed and handed down by a judge
divine: priest
The brain...the cripple: Portia is saying that although it is easy for the brain to work out what the body should do, a rush of emotions often takes over, making good advice look wrong. She uses the parallel of the hare, which seems to act crazily at mating time, managing to avoid the net set to trap it.
reasoning: discussion
in the fashion: of a kind
will: wishes and the will left by her father
over-name them: run through their names
level: make a guess

1 The gentleman from Naples boasts of his horsemanship and of his ability to shoe horses himself.

and yet for aught I see, they are as sick that surfeit
with too much, as they that starve with nothing. It
is no mean happiness therefore to be seated in the
mean; superfluity comes sooner by white hairs, but
competency lives longer.

PORTIA   Good sentences, and well pronounced.   10

NERISSA They would be better if well followed.

PORTIA   If to do were as easy as to know what were good to
do, chapels had been churches, and poor men's
cottages princes' palaces. It is a good divine that
follows his own instructions. I can easier teach twenty
what were good to be done, than be one of the
twenty to follow mine own teaching. The brain may
devise laws for the blood, but a hot temper leaps o'er
a cold decree; such a hare is madness the youth, to
skip o'er the meshes of good counsel the cripple.   20
But this reasoning is not in the fashion to choose me
a husband. O me, the word 'choose'! I may neither
choose whom I would, nor refuse whom I dislike; so
is the will of a living daughter curbed by the will of a
dead father. Is it not hard Nerissa, that I cannot
choose one, nor refuse none?

NERISSA Your father was ever virtuous, and holy men at their
death have good inspirations, therefore the lottery
that he hath devised in these three chests of gold,
silver, and lead, whereof who chooses his   30
meaning chooses you, will no doubt never be
chosen by any rightly, but one who shall rightly
love. But what warmth is there in your affection
towards any of these princely suitors that are already
come?

PORTIA   I pray thee over-name them, and as thou namest
them, I will describe them, and, according to my
description level at my affection.

NERISSA First there is the Neapolitan prince.

PORTIA   Ay that's a colt indeed, for he doth nothing but   40

Portia says what she thinks of her suitors. These opinions are largely in line with the stereotypical views of other nationalities common in Shakespeare's time.

2 County Palatine – a lord with powers of a king in his own lands. Portia finds he frowns all the time and cannot laugh, even at jokes. She would rather marry a skull than either of these two.

2 >

3 The French lord is a boaster, of sudden mood-swings. He dances about, he fences. He seems to be twenty men in one. Portia would never know where she was.

3 >

4 The English baron is handsome but speaks none of the languages that Portia knows, so they cannot communicate. His clothes are an unsuitable mixture of various foreign fashions and his behaviour is odd.

4 >

	talk of his horse, and he makes it a great appropriation to his own good parts that he can shoe him himself. I am much afeard my lady his mother played false with a smith.
NERISSA	Then there is the County Palatine.
PORTIA	He doth nothing but frown, as who should say, 'An you will not have me, choose'; he hears merry tales and smiles not; I fear he will prove the weeping philosopher when he grows old, being so full of unmannerly sadness in his youth. I had rather 50 be married to a death's-head with a bone in his mouth than to either of these. God defend me from these two.
NERISSA	How say you by the French lord, Monsieur Le Bon?
PORTIA	God made him, and therefore let him pass for a man. In truth I know it is a sin to be a mocker, but he–why he hath a horse better than the Neapolitan's; a better bad habit of frowning than the Count Palatine; he is every man in no man; 60 if a throstle sing, he falls straight a-capering; he will fence with his own shadow. If I should marry him, I should marry twenty husbands. If he would despise me, I would forgive him, for if he love me to madness, I shall never requite him.
NERISSA	What say you then to Falconbridge, the young baron of England?
PORTIA	You know I say nothing to him, for he understands not me, nor I him: he hath neither Latin, French, nor Italian and you will come into the court 70 and swear that I have a poor pennyworth in the English. He is a proper man's picture, but alas, who can converse with a dumb show? How oddly he is suited! I think he bought his doublet in Italy, his round hose in France, his bonnet in Germany, and his behaviour everywhere.

The list continues. Nerissa reveals they have all decided to go home without making the choice. Portia is determined to abide by her father's will.

5 >

---

5 Portia comments on the aggression between the Scotsman and the Englishman. (There were border skirmishes at the time of the play, and the French backed the Scots against the English.)

6 >

6 The young German behaves badly when he is sober and far worse when he is drunk. Portia suggests putting a glass of wine on one of the wrong caskets to influence his choice. She will not marry a drunkard.

by some other sort: in some other way
your father's imposition: the conditions your father set
Sibylla: in Greek and Roman legend the sibyls were oracles or prophetesses. The sibyl of Cumae asked Apollo for the gift of long life.
Diana: the moon-goddess, portrayed as a huntress and protector of virgins
parcel: group
dote on: am head-over-heels in love with

NERISSA	What think you of the Scottish lord his neighbour?
PORTIA	That he hath a neighbourly charity in him, for he borrowed a box of the ear of the Englishman, and swore he would pay him again when he was 80 able. I think the Frenchman became his surety and sealed under for another.
NERISSA	How like you the young German, the Duke of Saxony's nephew?
PORTIA	Very vilely in the morning when he is sober, and most vilely in the afternoon when he is drunk. When he is best, he is a little worse than a man, and when he is worst, he is little better than a beast. An the worst fall that ever fell, I hope I shall make shift to go without him. 90
NERISSA	If he should offer to choose, and choose the right casket, you should refuse to perform your father's will, if you should refuse to accept him.
PORTIA	Therefore for fear of the worse, I pray thee set a deep glass of rhenish wine on the contrary casket, for if the devil be within, and that temptation without, I know he will choose it. I will do any thing Nerissa, ere I'll be married to a sponge.
NERISSA	You need not fear, lady, the having any of these lords. They have acquainted me with their 100 determinations, which is indeed to return to their home, and to trouble you with no more suit, unless you may be won by some other sort than your father's imposition, depending on the caskets.
PORTIA	If I live to be as old as Sibylla, I will die as chaste as Diana, unless I be obtained by the manner of my father's will. I am glad this parcel of wooers are so reasonable, for there is not one among them but I dote on his very absence; and I pray God grant them a fair departure. 110
NERISSA	Do you not remember lady, in your father's time, a Venetian, a scholar and a soldier, that came

Nerissa mentions a visitor from when Portia's father was
alive. Portia remembers him favourably, and his name –
Bassanio. As the suitors leave, another is about to arrive.

1 The suitors just listed are about to take their leave. A
  messenger has come to announce that the Prince of
  Morocco will soon arrive.

2 Portia does not welcome the idea of this new suitor.

CTIVITIES

Keeping track

Scene 1

1 Antonio is depressed without knowing why. What two
  possible reasons do his friends suggest?
2 Do you think Gratiano's contributions help Antonio's mood?
3 What are your first impressions of Bassanio?
4 Is he in love?
5 Why does he need to borrow money again now?

hither in company of the Marquis of Montferrat?

PORTIA   Yes, yes, it was Bassanio, as I think, so was he called.

NERISSA   True madam, he of all the men that ever my foolish
           eyes looked upon, was the best deserving a fair lady.

PORTIA   I remember him well, and I remember him worthy
           of thy praise.

           Enter a Serving-man

           How now, what news?

SERVING-MAN   The four strangers seek for you madam to   120
               take their leave; and there is a forerunner come
               from a fifth, the Prince of Morocco, who brings
               word the prince his master will be here tonight.

PORTIA   If I could bid the fifth welcome with so good a
           heart as I can bid the other four farewell, I should
           be glad of his approach. If he have the condition of
           a saint, and the complexion of a devil, I had rather
           he should shrive me than wive me.
           Come Nerissa. Sirrah go before. Whiles we shut
           the gates upon one wooer, another knocks at   130
           the door.

                                                    [*Exeunt*

Scene 2

6 How do Portia's first words compare with Antonio's?
7 What is the reason for her mood?
8 Do you think Nerissa is a help to her?
9 Sum up, in a word or short phrase, Portia's attitude to her
   suitors so far.

Discussion

Friendship

1 Suppose you were Antonio in scene 1. If some of your friends tried to cheer you up, how would you react to their efforts?
2 a What are the qualities you expect in a friend?
  b Antonio and Bassanio are portrayed as good friends. Do they share any of these qualities? Make a note of them and add to this list as you progress through the play.
3 Look at the relationship between Portia and Nerissa. Does this friendship seem different from that between the two men? List any similarities and differences you find.

Marriage

Portia's father knew that when he died, Portia would be a very rich heiress. He devised the competition of the three caskets to try to ensure that only someone who really loved her for herself would marry her. He wanted to put off anyone who was just after her money.

1 Why is this arrangement making Portia irritated and unhappy?
2 Portia apparently has no say in choosing a husband.
  a How much freedom in choosing a marriage partner do people have nowadays?
  b What factors affect the choice of a marriage partner?
  c What do you believe should be the basis for a successful marriage?
3 The contest of the three caskets contains typical elements of a fairy story. What are these? Can you predict from your knowledge of fairy stories what might happen to Portia?

Drama

1 Imagine you are designers starting work on a production of *The Merchant of Venice*. Working in a group of five or six, produce some designs and ideas. You must be prepared to justify these with reference to the text. Here are some suggestions to start you thinking:

- This play has been set in various historical periods, including the present day. In what period would *you* set it?
- How would you get across the impression of
  a wealth
  b trading
  c Venice – or does it have to be Venice?
- Where is scene 1 set? Consider many different possibilities – for example, putting Antonio and friends in Antonio's warehouse; drinking in a bar; lounging in a Turkish bath; wandering round a busy market eating fruit or gambling in a casino.
- Many of these ideas suggest a large cast. What difference would it make if you had only a small company to draw on? Do any research you need and when you have gathered together some ideas and drawings, present them at a production meeting. Your drawings could include designs for several characters, costumes, sets for particular scenes, and perhaps stage props. Your teacher could take the role of producer.
2 Each of Portia's humorous descriptions of her suitors depicts a stereotype which we might consider slanderous. (A slanderous statement is an untrue statement that might damage a person's reputation.) Imagine that the young men find out what she has said about them and call their lawyers.
  - Divide the class into six groups.
  - Each group represents one of the six suitors.
  - Decide what you would say in court to defend your client's honour.
  - Read what Portia says about them and find a way to use her words to show your client in a better light.

Character

You will learn about the characters in the play from:
a what they say about themselves
b what they say about other people and events
c how they react to what people say to them
d what other people say about them.

In the first part of scene 1 **a** and **c** are the most important sources of information about Antonio.

1 Start a CHARACTER LOG for Antonio (see CHARACTER LOG on page 206). Note how Antonio's speeches are longer and seem warmer when he is alone with Bassanio.

2 Start CHARACTER LOGS also for Bassanio and for Portia and Nerissa. Note that Bassanio talks about Portia to Antonio, and that Portia reacts to the name 'Bassanio' when she remembers a previous brief meeting with him.

Close study

In scene 1 lines 119–121, Antonio asks Bassanio a question.
In scene 1 lines 161–166, Bassanio at last answers it.
Either individually, or with a partner, work out the following.

- What the question and answer are.
- What comes between the question and the answer.
- Why so many words are necessary.
- When love and money are mentioned together, which tends to come first? Give line references.
- Draw up a comprehensive list of all the words connected with money.

When a word such as 'owe' is used more than once, count the total number of times it is used and put the number beside it.

Writing

1 Antonio keeps a diary. As Antonio, write an entry in which you reflect upon your friendship with Bassanio. Explain why you are prepared to be so generous towards him.

2 The story of the caskets is a scoop for the *Belmont Bugle*. Write a front page article about it. Decide whether to use a style suitable for a tabloid newspaper or a broadsheet.

3 Either:
   a The same newspaper has a women's page on which topical issues concerning women are discussed. Several letters have been received about Portia's predicament. Write one of these letters, from someone who is opposed to the terms of her father's will.

Or:

b As Portia, write a letter to a friend in which you explain your predicament and how you feel about it.

Quiz

1 Name three dangers to shipping mentioned by Solanio and Salerio.
2 Name two possible cargoes in Antonio's ships.
3 Where is a second arrow likely to land?
4 Which two phrases tell us Portia is fair-haired?
5 'Shakespeare can't count' says someone after reading scene 2. Can you justify this outrageous statement?

Who says, and to whom:

6 '*Why then you are in love.*'
7 '*When you have them, they are not worth the search.*'
8 '*My ventures are not in one bottom trusted.*'
9 '*Yes, yes, it was Bassanio.*'
10 '*Your father was ever virtuous.*' ?

Bassanio has approached Shylock for a loan to Antonio. Shylock considers Antonio's circumstances and credit rating.

---

ducats: gold coins used in many European countries at this time.

well: yes, I see (he is considering the proposition)

become bound: guarantee the amount, be liable if Bassanio cannot repay the loan

may you stead me?: Can you help me?

pleasure: satisfy

good: 'good' for that amount of money and a 'good' person

imputation: suggestion

sufficient: able to guarantee the money

in supposition: unsure

Rialto: the Exchange or business centre in medieval and renaissance Venice where merchants met to agree deals

squandered abroad: scattered recklessly around

Be assured: do not doubt

Scene ③

Venice

Enter BASSANIO *and* SHYLOCK

SHYLOCK	Three thousand ducats–well.
BASSANIO	Ay sir, for three months.
SHYLOCK	For three months–well.
BASSANIO	For the which as I told you, Antonio shall be bound.
SHYLOCK	Antonio shall become bound–well.
BASSANIO	May you stead me? Will you pleasure me? Shall I know your answer?
SHYLOCK	Three thousand ducats for three months, and Antonio bound. 10
BASSANIO	Your answer to that.
SHYLOCK	Antonio is a good man.
BASSANIO	Have you heard any imputation to the contrary?
SHYLOCK	Ho no, no, no, no. My meaning in saying he is a good man, is to have you understand me that he is sufficient–yet his means are in supposition: he hath an argosy bound to Tripolis, another to the Indies; I understand moreover upon the Rialto, he hath a third at Mexico, a fourth for England, and other ventures he hath squandered abroad. But ships 20 are but boards, sailors but men; there be land-rats and water-rats, water-thieves and land-thieves, I mean pirates, and then there is the peril of waters, winds, and rocks. The man is notwithstanding sufficient. Three thousand ducats–I think I may take his bond.
BASSANIO	Be assured you may.

Antonio arrives. We learn of Shylock's hatred for him. Shylock suggests he may need to borrow in order to lend the money.

be assured: obtain guarantees

bethink me: consider the matter

habitation...into: When Jesus healed a man 'possessed by devils' he sent the devils into a herd of pigs which then rushed over a cliff into the sea. Jews traditionally do not eat pig-meat of any sort.

Nazarite: inhabitant of Nazareth (Jesus Christ)

fawning publican: cringeing tax-gatherer. 'Publicans' mentioned in the New Testament were Jews who gathered taxes from the Jewish population for their Roman rulers, and so were hated and despised.

low simplicity: simple folly

gratis: free, without demanding interest

usance: usury, the charging of interest on money loans

catch...hip: get a hold over him, get him at a disadvantage

ancient grudge: the traditional hostility between Jews and Christians apparently originating in the accusation that the Jews were responsible for killing Jesus Christ

rails on: complains bitterly about

thrift: profit

furnish me: provide it for me

signior: gentleman, form of address

SHYLOCK	I will be assured I may. And that I may be assured, I will bethink me. May I speak with Antonio?
BASSANIO	If it please you to dine with us. 30
SHYLOCK	Yes, to smell pork, to eat of the habitation which your prophet the Nazarite conjured the devil into. I will buy with you, sell with you, talk with you, walk with you, and so following. But I will not eat with you, drink with you, nor pray with you. What news on the Rialto? Who is he comes here?

Enter ANTONIO

BASSANIO	This is Signior Antonio.
SHYLOCK	[*Aside*] How like a fawning publican he looks.

I hate him for he is a Christian.
But more, for that in low simplicity 40
He lends out money gratis, and brings down
The rate of usance here with us in Venice.
If I can catch him once upon the hip,
I will feed fat the ancient grudge I bear him.
He hates our sacred nation, and he rails
Even there where merchants most do congregate,
On me, my bargains, and my well-won thrift,
Which he calls interest. Cursed be my tribe
If I forgive him.

BASSANIO	Shylock, do you hear?
SHYLOCK	I am debating of my present store, 50

And by the near guess of my memory
I cannot instantly raise up the gross
Of full three thousand ducats. What of that?
Tubal a wealthy Hebrew of my tribe,
Will furnish me. But soft, how many months
Do you desire? [*To Antonio*] Rest you fair good signior,
Your worship was the last man in our mouths.

ANTONIO	Shylock, although I neither lend nor borrow

By taking nor by giving of excess,

To justify shrewd dealing, Shylock tells the story of Jacob and Laban's sheep.

ripe: immediate
Is he yet possessed...?: Does he know yet...?
would: would like, want
Upon advantage: for interest
use it: make a practice of it

1 When Jacob and his uncle Laban had agreed that Jacob should have all the spotted and streaked sheep and goats in the flock, the ewes were put with the rams to mate.
2 Jacob peeled patches of the bark off thin branches and set up rows of them in front of the ewes.
3 For many centuries superstition had it that the unborn young could be affected by what the mother saw during pregnancy. Putting an object with dark and light patches in front of the ewes would ensure that many lambs would be patchily marked and therefore his.
4 Shylock is telling Antonio that Jacob's skill produced profit.
5 Antonio asserts this was not skill – it was ordained by God. It doesn't mean that the taking of interest is good.

	Yet to supply the ripe wants of my friend, 60
	I'll break a custom. Is he yet possessed
	How much ye would?
SHYLOCK	Ay, ay, three thousand ducats.
ANTONIO	And for three months.
SHYLOCK	I had forgot–three months, you told me so.
	Well then, your bond; and let me see–but hear you,
	Methought you said you neither lend nor borrow
	Upon advantage.
ANTONIO	I do never use it.
SHYLOCK	When Jacob grazed his uncle Laban's sheep–
	This Jacob from our holy Abram was,
	As his wise mother wrought in his behalf, 70
	The third possessor; ay, he was the third–
ANTONIO	And what of him? did he take interest?
SHYLOCK	No, not take interest, not as you would say
	Directly interest; mark what Jacob did.
	When Laban and himself were compromised
	That all the eanlings which were streaked and pied
	Should fall as Jacob's hire, the ewes being rank
	In end of autumn turned to the rams,
	And when the work of generation was
	Between these woolly breeders in the act, 80
	The skilful shepherd pilled me certain wands
	And in the doing of the deed of kind
	He stuck them up before the fulsome ewes,
	Who then conceiving, did in eaning time
	Fall parti-coloured lambs, and those were Jacob's.
	This was a way to thrive, and he was blest;
	And thrift is blessing if men steal it not.
ANTONIO	This was a venture sir, that Jacob served for,
	A thing not in his power to bring to pass,
	But swayed and fashioned by the hand of heaven. 90
	Was this inserted to make interest good?

Antonio mentions the devil and evil almost in the same breath as he tries to clinch the loan. Shylock speaks of the way Antonio treats him.

6 ▷

7 ▷

6 Shylock claims that his money can breed money.
7 Antonio says that the devil can quote the Bible for his own ends. Christians at this time were not allowed to lend money for interest.

8 Shylock returns to the question of the loan.

8 ▷

beholding: under an obligation, indebted
rated: reproved, scolded
usances: another word for the more usual 'usuries' – the taking of interest on a money loan
Still: always
sufferance: putting up with things, patience
gaberdine: ankle-length loose coat, worn by men, especially Jews, in the Middle Ages
Go to: an expression of amazement
did...rheum: spat
foot/spurn: kick, push me aside with your foot
suit: request
bondman's key: slave's voice

Or is your gold and silver ewes and rams?

SHYLOCK   I cannot tell, I make it breed as fast.
           But note me signior.

ANTONIO   Mark you this Bassanio,
           The devil can cite Scripture for his purpose.
           An evil soul producing holy witness
           Is like a villain with a smiling cheek,
           A goodly apple rotten at the heart.
           O what a goodly outside falsehood hath.

SHYLOCK   Three thousand ducats–'tis a good round sum.   100
           Three months from twelve–then let me see, the
               rate–

ANTONIO   Well Shylock, shall we be beholding to you?

SHYLOCK   Signior Antonio, many a time and oft
           In the Rialto you have rated me
           About my moneys and my usances.
           Still have I borne it with a patient shrug,
           For sufferance is the badge of all our tribe.
           You call me misbeliever, cut-throat dog,
           And spit upon my Jewish gaberdine,
           And all for use of that which is mine own.   110
           Well then, it now appears you need my help.
           Go to then, you come to me, and you say,
           'Shylock, we would have moneys'–you say so;
           You that did void your rheum upon my beard,
           And foot me as you spurn a stranger cur
           Over your threshold–moneys is your suit.
           What should I say to you? Should I not say,
           'Hath a dog money? Is it possible
           A cur can lend three thousand ducats?' Or
           Shall I bend low, and in a bondman's key   120
           With bated breath, and whispering humbleness
           Say this:
           'Fair sir, you spat on me on Wednesday last,
           You spurned me such a day, another time
           You called me dog; and for these courtesies

Shylock claims he does not want to prolong the quarrel but will lend without charging interest. He proposes the 'joke' forfeit of a pound of flesh. Antonio agrees, sure that his ships will come home first.

---

for when did...friend: it is not in the nature of friendship to take interest on money lent to a friend

break: fail to pay the money back on the agreed day

take no doit...moneys: and take not one penny of interest for my loan

kind: natural generosity, kindness

notary: solicitor

single bond: bond with only one condition attached

merry sport: merely as a joke

let the forfeit...for: let us decide that the pledge shall be

necessity: need

	I'll lend you thus much moneys'?
ANTONIO	I am as like to call thee so again,
	To spit on thee again, to spurn thee too.
	If thou wilt lend this money, lend it not
	As to thy friends, for when did friendship take 130
	A breed of barren metal of his friend?
	But lend it rather to thine enemy,
	Who if he break, thou mayst with better face
	Exact the penalty.
SHYLOCK	Why look you how you storm.
	I would be friends with you, and have your love,
	Forget the shames that you have stained me with,
	Supply your present wants, and take no doit
	Of usance for my moneys–and you'll not hear me.
	This is kind I offer.
BASSANIO	This were kindness.
SHYLOCK	This kindness will I show– 140
	Go with me to a notary, seal me there
	Your single bond, and in a merry sport,
	If you repay me not on such a day,
	In such a place, such sum or sums as are
	Expressed in the condition, let the forfeit
	Be nominated for an equal pound
	Of your fair flesh, to be cut off and taken
	In what part of your body pleaseth me.
ANTONIO	Content, i'faith, I'll seal to such a bond,
	And say there is much kindness in the Jew. 150
BASSANIO	You shall not seal to such a bond for me,
	I'll rather dwell in my necessity.
ANTONIO	Why fear not man, I will not forfeit it.
	Within these two months, that's a month before
	This bond expires, I do expect return
	Of thrice three times the value of this bond.
SHYLOCK	O father Abram, what these Christians are,
	Whose own hard dealings teaches them suspect
	The thoughts of others. Pray you tell me this,

Shylock insists there is no advantage for him in this strange bond. They arrange to meet at the solicitor's. Bassanio does not like this forfeit.

exaction: demanding
fearful: timid
unthrifty knave: careless, good-for-nothing servant
presently: immediately
Hie thee: make haste

	If he should break his day, what should I gain	160
	By the exaction of the forfeiture?	
	A pound of man's flesh taken from a man	
	Is not so estimable, profitable neither,	
	As flesh of muttons, beefs, or goats. I say,	
	To buy his favour, I extend this friendship.	
	If he will take it, so; if not, adieu,	
	And for my love I pray you wrong me not.	
ANTONIO	Yes Shylock, I will seal unto this bond.	
SHYLOCK	Then meet me forthwith at the notary's.	
	Give him direction for this merry bond,	170
	And I will go and purse the ducats straight,	
	See to my house, left in the fearful guard	
	Of an unthrifty knave; and presently	
	I will be with you.	
ANTONIO	Hie thee gentle Jew.	

[*Exit Shylock*

	The Hebrew will turn Christian, he grows kind.
BASSANIO	I like not fair terms, and a villain's mind.
ANTONIO	Come on, in this there can be no dismay,
	My ships come home a month before the day.

[*Exeunt*

The Prince of Morocco arrives to choose between the caskets. He speaks proudly of his colour, but fears it may bother Portia. She reassures him.

Flourish Cornets: fanfare of trumpets
tawny: light brown
train: attendants
Mislike me...complexion: do not dislike me for my colour
shadowed livery: dark uniform (the colour of his skin)
burnished: brightly shining
near bred: closely related
Phoebus: the sun (god)
make incision: make a cut in our skin
aspect: appearance
Hath...valiant: made the bravest men afraid
By nice...eyes: by a fussy insistence on appearances alone
lottery of my destiny: the fact that my fate is to be decided by chance
scanted...wit: restricted me by both his will and wisdom.
Portia is claiming that his colour does not matter to her. If her father had not set up the three caskets method of choosing her husband for her, then the Prince of Morocco would still have stood an equal chance with any of the suitors she has seen so far.

Act two

Scene 1

Belmont

Flourish Cornets. Enter the PRINCE OF MOROCCO *(a tawny Moor all in white) and three or four followers accordingly; with* PORTIA, NERISSA, *and their train*

MOROCCO   Mislike me not for my complexion,
The shadowed livery of the burnished sun,
To whom I am a neighbour, and near bred.
Bring me the fairest creature northward born,
Where Phoebus' fire scarce thaws the icicles,
And let us make incision for your love,
To prove whose blood is reddest, his or mine.
I tell thee lady, this aspect of mine
Hath feared the valiant. By my love I swear
The best-regarded virgins of our clime   10
Have loved it too. I would not change this hue,
Except to steal your thoughts, my gentle queen.

PORTIA   In terms of choice I am not solely led
By nice direction of a maiden's eyes;
Besides, the lottery of my destiny
Bars me the right of voluntary choosing.
But if my father had not scanted me,
And hedged me by his wit to yield myself
His wife who wins me by that means I told you,
Yourself, renowned prince, then stood as fair   20
As any comer I have looked on yet
For my affection.

MOROCCO   Even for that I thank you.
Therefore I pray you lead me to the caskets

The Prince gives some account of his bravery but recognizes it can count for nothing when it is chance which will decide.

1 He has killed the Shah of Persia in battle and a Persian prince, himself successful in war.
2 He would dare any brave deed to win Portia, taking cubs from a she-bear, braving a hungry lion.
3 But he knows that if Hercules, however brave and strong, and his servant were to play at dice, the weaker man might just as easily win. This is what he faces.

4 Portia leads him away to the temple to take the oath that if he fails in his choice he must never afterwards seek to marry.

ACTIVITIES

Keeping track

Act 1 scene 3

1 Shylock is a moneylender. Does he seem eager to do business with Bassanio?

To try my fortune. By this scimitar
That slew the Sophy, and a Persian prince
That won three fields of Sultan Solyman,
I would o'erstare the sternest eyes that look,
Outbrave the heart most daring on the earth,
Pluck the young sucking cubs from the she-bear,
Yea, mock the lion when he roars for prey,   30
To win thee lady. But, alas the while,
If Hercules and Lichas play at dice
Which is the better man, the greater throw
May turn by fortune from the weaker hand:
So is Alcides beaten by his rage,
And so may I, blind Fortune leading me,
Miss that which one unworthier may attain,
And die with grieving.

PORTIA   You must take your chance,
And either not attempt to choose at all;
Or swear before you choose, if you choose
     wrong   40
Never to speak to lady afterward
In way of marriage. Therefore be advised.

MOROCCO   Nor will not. Come bring me unto my chance.

PORTIA   First forward to the temple, after dinner
Your hazard shall be made.

MOROCCO   Good fortune then,
To make me blest or cursed'st among men.
                                    [*Cornets. Exeunt*

2 Which does Shylock think is safer, his business or Antonio's?
3 Why doesn't Shylock want to dine with Bassanio and
     Antonio?

4 What strict principle of his is Antonio breaking to help
   Bassanio? (lines 58–62, 66–67)
5 Shylock tells a Bible story to try to prove that the taking of
   profit is blessed, as long as thieving is not involved. Does he
   convince Antonio?
6 Shylock accuses Antonio of a whole catalogue of nastiness.
   How does Antonio answer the charges?
7 How does Bassanio react to the proposed bond?

Act 2 scene 1

8 We have watched racial and religious tensions at work in Act 1
   scene 3. The Prince of Morocco opens Act 2 scene 1 with
   another sensitive issue. What is it?
9 If Antonio loses his gamble, he must forfeit a pound of flesh.
   What must Portia's suitors give up if they fail to win her?

Discussion

1 • Shylock practises 'usury'. What exactly do you understand
     by this? (Look at the note on page 28 and at page 218.)
   • Antonio is a rich merchant – how exactly does he make his
     money?
   • Shylock and Antonio 'make money work' to make more
     money. What kind of work might they be doing today?
2 Why do Antonio and Shylock hate each other?
3 Look at Act 1 scene 3 lines 103–126 in which Shylock
   describes the way Antonio has treated him. Jot down the
   insulting things that Antonio has called Shylock. How would
   you react if someone continually called you names?
4 Why does Shylock agree to lend Antonio money?
5 In Act 2 scene 1 we meet the Moroccan prince. Read Portia's
   speech: '*In terms of choice...*' (line 13). What do you think is
   her real opinion of the prince? Do you think she may have
   been influenced by the would-be suitors she has met so far?

Drama

1 Using the information you gain in Act 1 scene 3, 'hotseat'

Shylock and Antonio (page 208). Use this device to explore their mutual hatred.

2 Consider the characters of Shylock and Antonio.
  A useful rehearsal technique is to decide what animal could represent each character.
  • If you have space you could practise moving as that animal.
  • If not, draw the character as half human, half chosen animal. You can develop this device by thinking about what kind of car, house, or music would best represent each character.

3 Another point in the play where Shakespeare challenges his audience's prejudices is the arrival of the Prince of Morocco. This needs to be a great spectacle but we must also be aware of Portia's distaste for her suitor.
  • You are the costume designers for a production of the play.
  • The director has not yet set the play in any specific period and is open to suggestions.
  • He is concerned to portray the Prince with some dignity.
  • He is not very sympathetic to the character of Portia.
  • The production is for a theatre in a culturally diverse city.
  • The cast will include actors from different ethnic backgrounds.
  Working in a team of five or six, produce drawings and ideas for this scene. You must be prepared to justify your designs to your teacher, as the director, with reference to the text.

Character

1 When we first meet Antonio he is at leisure, surrounded by friends. When we first meet Shylock he is at work, with a client. We learn about Antonio gradually, in the ways mentioned in CHARACTER after Act 1 scenes 1, 2. We now learn about Shylock in an 'aside'. This is a speech directly to the audience, with many of the qualities of a 'thought bubble' in a picture story or comic. Because no-one except the audience is listening to the aside there is no pretence in it; it reveals exactly what Shylock thinks.

Start your CHARACTER LOG for Shylock. Think about the following points:
- Does the use of the 'aside' necessarily mean that Shylock is a straightforward character?
- How do you interpret Shylock 'forgetting' the period of the loan? Look at Act 1 scene 3 lines 3, 9, 55–56, 64.
- Shylock goes out of his way to try to persuade Antonio that it is all right to take interest. What might this suggest about his character?
- Shylock tells Antonio directly what he dislikes about his behaviour to him.

2 Add to your CHARACTER LOG for Bassanio. What do the three short questions in Act 1 scene 3 lines 7 and 8 tell us about his state of mind? What do we learn about him in scene 3 lines 151–152 and line 176?

3 Add to your CHARACTER LOG for Portia. Look carefully at Act 2 scene 1 lines 20–22. She is reassuring the Prince about her attitude to his colour. How reassured would the Prince be if he knew what we have heard Portia say about her other suitors?

Close study

Act 1 scene 3

Read Shylock's speech, lines 103–126. Antonio's request for money has given Shylock the only chance he has ever had to confront – although only in private – the man who has often humiliated him in public. Look at the pattern of the speech and the variety in it.

1 Antonio hopes to close the deal. What question does he ask to help him do this? What answer does he get, eventually?

2 Consider the various uses Shakespeare makes of repetition. What effect do they have?

3 How many times is 'you' used in the first eight lines? How many times in the next eight? What does the slow build-up and then this quick-fire repetition tell us about Shylock's mood?

4 Similarly, count the number of times 'money' or 'moneys' is

mentioned in the speech. How does it compare with the
number of times words meaning 'dog' are used. What
conclusions do you draw from this?

5 How would you describe Shylock's use of the word '*courtesies*'
(line 125)? What should a gentleman like Antonio feel about
his 'courteous' behaviour?

6 Shylock asks several rhetorical questions, questions which do
not expect an answer. What kind of voice do you think would
be best for these?

  Think about how an actor is helped by this writing to vary
the pace, the intensity, the tone and the pitch of this speech.
Work with a partner and practise saying this speech aloud.

Writing

1 You are leaning on the Rialto bridge, idly watching the water
below. People passing by are gossiping about the latest news:
Antonio is borrowing money from Shylock and has made a
very strange agreement with him. Different people are reacting
in different ways. For example, you might overhear
conversations involving: two of Antonio's warehouse workers,
dock workers, Bassanio and a friend, a banker, someone who
has invested in one of Antonio's ships. Write the snippets of
conversation you hear as they pass.

2 Tubal, Shylock's friend, has heard about the loan to Antonio.
He is amazed that Shylock should have lent money to this man
of all people. Write the speech in which Shylock explains to
Tubal the reasons for his actions.

Quiz

1 We know already that there are three caskets. In what two ways
does this number feature in Act 1 scene 3?

2 There is a breed of sheep today called Jacob's sheep. How are
they different from other breeds?

3 How does Shylock 'breed' money?

4 In how many months' time is Antonio expecting his ships to
return?

5 How much flesh will Shylock be able to claim from Antonio?

Launcelot Gobbo is having a battle with his conscience about whether to leave Shylock's service. He wants to go, but duty is telling him to stay.

will serve me: must allow me

fiend: devil

as aforesaid: as mentioned earlier (a rather pompous-sounding legal term)

pack: go off

Fia!: Forward!

hanging about the neck of: holding back (his conscience is trying to stop his heart taking action)

something: somewhat, rather

smack: have a trace of, or kiss noisily

grow to: lean towards

God bless the mark: the 'mark' was possibly a reference to the cross and this remark was supposed to protect the speaker after a mention of the devil.

saving your reverence: of similar force to the previous remark, a polite apology.

incarnation: Launcelot's mistake for 'incarnate' – in bodily form.

Scene ②

Venice

Enter LAUNCELOT

LAUNCELOT   Certainly my conscience will serve me to run from
this Jew my master. The fiend is at mine elbow, and
tempts me, saying to me, 'Gobbo, Launcelot
Gobbo, good Launcelot', or 'Good Gobbo', or
'Good Launcelot Gobbo, use your legs, take the
start, run away'. My conscience says, 'No, take heed
honest Launcelot, take heed honest Gobbo', or as
aforesaid, 'Honest Launcelot Gobbo; do not run,
scorn running with thy heels'. Well, the most
courageous fiend bids me pack: 'Fia!' says the   10
fiend; 'Away!' says the fiend; 'For the heavens,
rouse up a brave mind', says the fiend, 'and run.'
Well, my conscience, hanging about the neck of my
heart, says very wisely to me: 'My honest friend
Launcelot, being an honest man's son', or rather an
honest woman's son–for indeed my father did
something smack, something grow to, he had a
kind of taste–well, my conscience says, 'Launcelot
budge not'. 'Budge', says the fiend. 'Budge not',
says my conscience. 'Conscience', say I, 'you   20
counsel well.' 'Fiend', say I, 'you counsel well.' To
be ruled by my conscience, I should stay with the
Jew my master, who–God bless the mark–is a kind
of devil; and to run away from the Jew I should be
ruled by the fiend, who–saving your reverence–is
the devil himself. Certainly the Jew is the very devil
incarnation, and in my conscience, my conscience is
but a kind of hard conscience, to offer to counsel
me to stay with the Jew. The fiend gives the more
friendly counsel. I will run, fiend; my heels are   30
at your command, I will run.

Launcelot's father is looking for Shylock's house, to find his son. Launcelot deliberately confuses the old man and then tells him his son is dead.

1 Launcelot recognizes his father, who, old and nearly blind, asks him the way to Shylock's house, where he hopes to find Launcelot.

2 Launcelot amuses himself at the old man's expense, giving him deliberately confusing directions.

3 The son refers to himself as 'Master Launcelot'. The old man will not allow this as they are poor people.

4 After more teasing Launcelot goes on to tell old Gobbo that his son is dead. This really distresses the old man.

Enter OLD GOBBO *with a basket*

GOBBO   Master young man, you I pray you, which is the
             way to master Jew's?

LAUNCELOT   [*Aside*] O heavens, this is my true-begotten father,
             who being more than sand-blind, high-gravel blind,
             knows me not–I will try confusions with him.

GOBBO   Master young gentleman, I pray you which is
             the way to master Jew's?

LAUNCELOT   Turn up on your right hand at the next turning, but
             at the next turning of all on your left; marry at   40
             the very next turning turn of no hand, but turn
             down indirectly to the Jew's house.

GOBBO   By God's sonties 'twill be a hard way to hit. Can
             you tell me whether one Launcelot that dwells with
             him, dwell with him or no?

LAUNCELOT   Talk you of young Master Launcelot? [*Aside*] Mark
             me now, now will I raise the waters. Talk you of
             young Master Launcelot?

GOBBO   No master sir, but a poor man's son. His father,
             though I say it, is an honest exceeding poor   50
             man, and God be thanked, well to live.

LAUNCELOT   Well, let his father be what 'a will, we talk of young
             Master Launcelot.

GOBBO   Your worship's friend and Launcelot sir.

LAUNCELOT   But I pray you, ergo old man, ergo I beseech you,
             talk you of young Master Launcelot?

GOBBO   Of Launcelot an't please your mastership.

LAUNCELOT   Ergo Master Launcelot. Talk not of Master
             Launcelot father; for the young gentleman–
             according to Fates and Destinies and such odd   60
             sayings, the Sisters Three and such branches of
             learning–is indeed deceased, or, as you would say in
             plain terms, gone to heaven.

GOBBO   Marry God forbid, the boy was the very staff of my

Launcelot now takes pity on his father and admits he is his son. The old man takes some convincing.

5 In his distress old Gobbo demands to know whether his son is alive or dead, declaring he is nearly blind. ⟨5⟩

6 Launcelot asks for his father's blessing. He mentions his mother's name to convince his father. ⟨6⟩

7 When Launcelot kneels for the blessing, he kneels back to front so that his father thinks his hair is a full beard. ⟨7⟩

8 Old Gobbo asks how Launcelot and his master are getting on. He has brought a present for Shylock. ⟨8⟩

	age, my very prop.
LAUNCELOT	Do I look like a cudgel, or a hovel-post, a staff, or a prop? Do you know me father?
GOBBO	Alack the day, I know you not young gentleman, but I pray you tell me, is my boy–God rest his soul –alive or dead? 70
LAUNCELOT	Do you not know me father?
GOBBO	Alack sir I am sand-blind, I know you not.
LAUNCELOT	Nay indeed, if you had your eyes, you might fail of the knowing me: it is a wise father that knows his own child. [*Kneels*] Well, old man, I will tell you news of your son–give me your blessing–truth will come to light. Murder cannot be hid long, a man's son may, but at the length truth will out.
GOBBO	Pray you, sir, stand up. I am sure you are not Launcelot, my boy. 80
LAUNCELOT	Pray you, let's have no more fooling about it, but give me your blessing. I am Launcelot your boy that was, your son that is, your child that shall be.
GOBBO	I cannot think you are my son.
LAUNCELOT	I know not what I shall think of that; but I am Launcelot the Jew's man, and I am sure Margery your wife is my mother.
GOBBO	Her name is Margery indeed. I'll be sworn if thou be Launcelot, thou art mine own flesh and blood. Lord worshipped might he be, what a beard hast 90 thou got; thou hast got more hair on thy chin than Dobbin my fill-horse has on his tail.
LAUNCELOT	It should seem then that Dobbin's tail grows backward. I am sure he had more hair of this tail than I have of my face when I last saw him.
GOBBO	Lord how art thou changed. How dost thou and thy master agree? I have brought him a present. How 'gree you now?

Launcelot admits he has decided to seek a new master. Bassanio is his choice and, when he enters, both father and son put Launcelot's case.

---

set up... run away: staked everything on running away
some ground: quite a distance
very: thorough, complete, true
halter: noose
you may tell...ribs: Launcelot, claiming he has become thin in the Jew's service, gets 'finger' and 'ribs' the wrong way round. He often confuses words and here the comic effect could be emphasized on stage by Launcelot spreading his fingers down his ribs and getting his blind father to feel how bony they are.
rare: splendid
liveries: servants' uniforms
anon: shortly
Gramercy: God bless your worship
aught: anything
infection: Gobbo means 'affection'
cater cousins: good friends
frutify: he means 'notify'

LAUNCELOT   Well, well, but for mine own part, as I have set up
my rest to run away, so I will not rest till I have   100
run some ground. My master's a very Jew. Give him
a present? Give him a halter. I am famished in his
service; you may tell every finger I have with my
ribs. Father, I am glad you are come, give me your
present to one Master Bassanio, who indeed gives
rare new liveries. If I serve not him, I will run as far
as God has any ground. O rare fortune, here comes
the man. To him father, for I am a Jew if I serve the
Jew any longer.

Enter BASSANIO *with* LEONARDO *and a follower or
two*

BASSANIO   You may do so, but let it be so hasted that   110
supper be ready at the farthest by five of the clock.
See these letters delivered, put the liveries to making,
and desire Gratiano to come anon to my lodging.
                                  [*Exit a Servant*

LAUNCELOT   To him father.

GOBBO   God bless your worship.

BASSANIO   Gramercy, wouldst thou aught with me?

GOBBO   Here's my son sir, a poor boy–

LAUNCELOT   Not a poor boy sir, but the rich Jew's man that
would sir–as my father shall specify–

GOBBO   He hath a great infection sir, as one would say,   120
to serve–

LAUNCELOT   Indeed the short and the long is, I serve the Jew,
and have a desire–as my father shall specify–

GOBBO   His master and he–saving your worship's reverence
–are scarce cater cousins–

LAUNCELOT   To be brief, the very truth is that the Jew, having
done me wrong, doth cause me–as my father, being
I hope an old man, shall frutify unto you–

Bassanio takes Launcelot on. Launcelot, with his father, goes to take his leave of Shylock.

impertinent: he means 'pertinent' – relevant
defect: he means 'effect'
preferred: recommended
preferment: promotion

1 Bassanio tells Launcelot to find his house and orders a splendid uniform for him.

2 Launcelot predicts a fine future for himself. He follows this with a nonsensical 'reading' of his palm and forecast of his fortunes.

3 Launcelot and old Gobbo depart. Launcelot must give notice to Shylock.

GOBBO	I have here a dish of doves that I would bestow
	upon your worship, and my suit is– 130
LAUNCELOT	In very brief, the suit is impertinent to myself, as
	your worship shall know by this honest old man,
	and though I say it, though old man, yet poor man,
	my father.
BASSANIO	One speak for both. What would you?
LAUNCELOT	Serve you sir.
GOBBO	That is the very defect of the matter sir.
BASSANIO	I know thee well, thou hast obtained thy suit.
	Shylock thy master spoke with me this day,
	And hath preferred thee, if it be preferment 140
	To leave a rich Jew's service, to become
	The follower of so poor a gentleman.
LAUNCELOT	The old proverb is very well parted between my
	master Shylock and you sir: you have the grace of
	God sir, and he hath enough.
BASSANIO	Thou speak'st it well. Go father with thy son.
	Take leave of thy old master, and inquire
	My lodging out. Give him a livery
	More guarded than his fellows'. See it done.
LAUNCELOT	Father in. I cannot get a service, no, I have 150
	ne'er a tongue in my head. Well, if any man in Italy
	have a fairer table which doth offer to swear upon a
	book, I shall have good fortune. Go to, here's a
	simple line of life, here's a small trifle of wives. Alas,
	fifteen wives is nothing, eleven widows and nine
	maids is a simple coming-in for one man; and then
	to 'scape drowning thrice, and to be in peril of my
	life with the edge of a feather-bed, here are simple
	scapes. Well, if Fortune be a woman, she's a good
	wench for this gear. Father come; I'll take my 160
	leave of the Jew in the twinkling.
	[*Exeunt Launcelot and old Gobbo*
BASSANIO	I pray thee, good Leonardo, think on this.

Gratiano wants to accompany Bassanio to Belmont.
Bassanio is not keen as he finds Gratiano rather loud and
rough, and his future may depend on the impression he
makes on Portia. Gratiano promises to behave.

4   Bassanio is giving a feast for his friends that evening.

Yonder: over there
suit: request
rude: uncivilized, rough
Parts: qualities
become: suit
liberal: freely
allay: repress, subdue
misconstrued: misinterpreted, misunderstood
habit: appearance, behaviour
grace: a short prayer before a meal asking God's blessing on
    the food and those about to eat
well studied...grandam: with considerable practice in
    appearing grave to please his grandmother

These things being bought and orderly bestowed,
Return in haste, for I do feast tonight
My best-esteemed acquaintance; hie thee, go.

LEONARDO   My best endeavours shall be done herein.

Enter GRATIANO

GRATIANO   Where is your master?

LEONARDO   Yonder sir he walks.   [*Exit*

GRATIANO   Signior Bassanio.

BASSANIO   Gratiano.

GRATIANO   I have a suit to you.

BASSANIO   You have obtained it.   170

GRATIANO   You must not deny me, I must go with you to
                 Belmont.

BASSANIO   Why then you must. But hear thee Gratiano,
                 Thou art too wild, too rude and bold of voice,
                 Parts that become thee happily enough,
                 And in such eyes as ours appear not faults,
                 But where thou art not known, why there they
                     show
                 Something too liberal. Pray thee take pain
                 To allay with some cold drops of modesty
                 Thy skipping spirit, lest through thy wild behaviour
                 I be misconstrued in the place I go to,   180
                 And lose my hopes.

GRATIANO   Signior Bassanio, hear me:
                 If I do not put on a sober habit,
                 Talk with respect, and swear but now and then,
                 Wear prayer-books in my pocket, look demurely,
                 Nay more, while grace is saying hood mine eyes
                 Thus with my hat, and sigh and say, 'amen';
                 Use all the observance of civility
                 Like one well studied in a sad ostent
                 To please his grandam, never trust me more.

BASSANIO   Well, we shall see your bearing.   190

Bassanio parts from Gratiano, who promises to join his party that evening with Lorenzo.

I bar tonight: I'm not counting tonight
gauge: judge
were: would be a
I would entreat...mirth: I would prefer you to be the life and soul of the party
purpose merriment: intend to have a good time

At Shylock's house, Launcelot is saying goodbye to Jessica. She hands him a letter for Lorenzo, whom she is going to marry.

---

exhibit: he probably means 'inhibit' – prevent his tongue from saying what he felt
pagan: heathen. It also meant 'prostitute'.
heinous: hateful, infamous
manners: morals

GRATIANO	Nay but I bar tonight, you shall not gauge me By what we do tonight.
BASSANIO	No that were pity. I would entreat you rather to put on Your boldest suit of mirth, for we have friends That purpose merriment. But fare you well, I have some business.
GRATIANO	And I must to Lorenzo and the rest. But we will visit you at supper-time. [*Exeunt*

Scene 3

Venice

Enter JESSICA *and* LAUNCELOT

JESSICA	I am sorry thou wilt leave my father so: Our house is hell, and thou, a merry devil, Didst rob it of some taste of tediousness. But fare thee well, there is a ducat for thee; And Launcelot, soon at supper shalt thou see Lorenzo, who is thy new master's guest. Give him this letter, do it secretly, And so farewell: I would not have my father See me in talk with thee.
LAUNCELOT	Adieu, tears exhibit my tongue. Most beautiful 10 pagan, most sweet Jew, if a Christian do not play the knave and get thee, I am much deceived. But adieu: these foolish drops do something drown my manly spirit. Adieu. [*Exit Launcelot*
JESSICA	Farewell good Launcelot. Alack, what heinous sin is it in me To be ashamed to be my father's child. But though I am a daughter to his blood, I am not to his manners. O Lorenzo If thou keep promise, I shall end this strife, 20 Become a Christian and thy loving wife. [*Exit*

Lorenzo and friends are planning their arrangements for the masque that evening. Launcelot gives Lorenzo the letter from Jessica and he sends a message in return.

1 Lorenzo suggests to his three friends that after Bassanio's meal they slip out and come back for the dancing in costume, wearing masks and with torchbearers.

⟩1⟩

2 Launcelot hands Lorenzo the letter from Jessica. Lorenzo recognizes the writing.

⟩2⟩

3 Launcelot is about to leave, to invite Shylock to Bassanio's feast.

⟩3⟩

4 Lorenzo asks him to tell Jessica secretly that he will do as she suggests. He links his need for a torchbearer with Jessica's disguise for her elopement with him.

⟩4⟩

Scene 4

Venice

Enter GRATIANO, LORENZO, SALERIO, *and* SOLANIO

LORENZO   Nay, we will slink away in supper-time,
Disguise us at my lodging and return,
All in an hour.

GRATIANO   We have not made good preparation.

SALERIO   We have not spoke us yet of torch-bearers.

SOLANIO   'Tis vile unless it may be quaintly ordered,
And better in my mind not undertook.

LORENZO   'Tis now but four o'clock, we have two hours
To furnish us.

Enter LAUNCELOT *with a letter*

             Friend Launcelot what's the news?

LAUNCELOT   An it shall please you to break up this, it shall   10
seem to signify.

LORENZO   I know the hand. In faith 'tis a fair hand,
And whiter than the paper it writ on
Is the fair hand that writ.

GRATIANO   Love-news in faith.

LAUNCELOT   By your leave sir.

LORENZO   Whither goest thou?

LAUNCELOT   Marry sir to bid my old master the Jew to sup
tonight with my new master the Christian.

LORENZO   Hold here, take this. Tell gentle Jessica
I will not fail her; speak it privately.   20
Go gentlemen,   [*Exit Launcelot*
Will you prepare you for this masque tonight?
I am provided of a torch-bearer.

SALERIO   Ay marry, I'll be gone about it straight.

Lorenzo tells Gratiano of Jessica's arrangements to provide herself with a disguise and with money.

5

5   The four men arrange to meet in an hour's time at Gratiano's lodging.

furnished: provided
page's suit: Jessica intends to elope dressed as a page boy
gentle: noble, with a possible play on words: 'gentile' – since Jessica is to marry a Christian
cross her foot: cross her path
Unless she do it: 'she' in this line refers to 'misfortune'
issue: child
faithless: unbelieving
peruse this: read this through

Shylock and Launcelot take leave of one another.

gormandize: eat greedily
rend...out: let your clothes get torn
was wont to tell me: used to tell me all the time

SOLANIO	And so will I.
LORENZO	Meet me and Gratiano At Gratiano's lodging some hour hence.
SALERIO	'Tis good we do so. [*Exeunt Salerio and Solanio*
GRATIANO	Was not that letter from fair Jessica?
LORENZO	I must needs tell thee all. She hath directed How I shall take her from her father's house, 30 What gold and jewels she is furnished with, What page's suit she hath in readiness. If e'er the Jew her father come to heaven, It will be for his gentle daughter's sake. And never dare misfortune cross her foot, Unless she do it under this excuse, That she is issue to a faithless Jew. Come go with me, peruse this as thou goest. Fair Jessica shall be my torch-bearer. [*Exeunt*

Scene 5

Venice

Enter SHYLOCK *and* LAUNCELOT

SHYLOCK	Well, thou shalt see, thy eyes shall be thy judge, The difference of old Shylock and Bassanio– What Jessica!–thou shalt not gormandize As thou hast done with me–What Jessica! And sleep, and snore, and rend apparel out– Why Jessica, I say!
LAUNCELOT	Why Jessica!
SHYLOCK	Who bids thee call? I do not bid thee call.
LAUNCELOT	Your worship was wont to tell me I could do nothing without bidding.

Enter JESSICA

JESSICA	Call you? What is your will? 10

Shylock does not want to dine with Bassanio – he is even more reluctant when he hears about the masque. Jessica is instructed to shut up the house and stay indoors. Launcelot delivers Lorenzo's message to her.

---

prodigal: lavish, wasteful

rest: peace of mind

For...tonight: a dream about money was supposed to mean bad luck

reproach: Launcelot means 'approach' but in line 21 Shylock picks up what he actually says

masque: usually a play or pantomime with music and dancing in a private house

Black Monday: Easter Monday. Launcelot gives a nonsensical horoscope to fit in with Shylock's dreams and fears.

wry-necked fife: flute-player with twisted neck (unavoidable while playing the flute)

Clamber...casements: do not climb up to the windows

varnished: painted, or masked

shallow foppery: foolish larking about

sirrah: form of address to a servant

Hagar's offspring: Ishmael, Abraham's son by Hagar, an Egyptian slave, was a gentile and an outcast.

patch: fool

profit: benefit, usefulness

SHYLOCK	I am bid forth to supper Jessica;
	There are my keys. But wherefore should I go?
	I am not bid for love, they flatter me.
	But yet I'll go in hate, to feed upon
	The prodigal Christian. Jessica my girl,
	Look to my house. I am right loath to go,
	There is some ill a-brewing towards my rest,
	For I did dream of money bags tonight.
LAUNCELOT	I beseech you sir, go. My young master doth expect
	your reproach. 20
SHYLOCK	So do I his.
LAUNCELOT	And they have conspired together–I will not say you
	shall see a masque, but if you do, then it was not for
	nothing that my nose fell a-bleeding on Black
	Monday last, at six o'clock i' the morning, falling
	out that year on Ash-Wednesday was four year in
	th'afternoon.
SHYLOCK	What, are there masques? Hear you me Jessica:
	Lock up my doors, and when you hear the drum
	And the vile squealing of the wry-necked fife, 30
	Clamber not you up to the casements then,
	Nor thrust your head into the public street
	To gaze on Christian fools with varnished faces.
	But stop my house's ears, I mean my casements,
	Let not the sound of shallow foppery enter
	My sober house. By Jacob's staff, I swear
	I have no mind of feasting forth tonight.
	But I will go. Go you before me sirrah,
	Say I will come.
LAUNCELOT	I will go before, sir. Mistress, look out at window 40
	for all this–
	There will come a Christian by
	Will be worth a Jewes' eye. [*Exit*
SHYLOCK	What says that fool of Hagar's offspring, ha?
JESSICA	His words were, 'Farewell mistress', nothing else.
SHYLOCK	The patch is kind enough, but a huge feeder,
	Snail-slow in profit, and he sleeps by day

Shylock goes off to dine with Bassanio, unaware that Jessica is about to elope with a Christian.

wildcat: the wildcat is a nocturnal animal and so sleeps by day
Drones: male honey-bees, non-workers
Fast bind, fast find: what is firmly shut up will stay secure

Lorenzo's friends are waiting for him. He is late.

penthouse: overhanging upper storey of a house (in Elizabethan England, not in Venice)
he out-dwells his hour: he is late
O ten...unforfeited: The doves of Venus (Roman goddess of love) fly much faster to a couple who have just fallen in love than to those in a long engagement.
holds: holds true
untread again...first?: paces home again with the untired energy with which he first stepped out
younger: younger son
prodigal: spendthrift (younger son) of the parable in the Bible (*Luke 15, 11–32*)
scarfed bark: ship decorated with flags and pennants
strumpet: prostitute
overweathered: weather-beaten
ribs: the ship's timbers and the skinny son's ribs
rent: torn

More than the wildcat. Drones hive not with me,
Therefore I part with him, and part with him
To one that I would have him help to waste   50
His borrowed purse. Well Jessica, go in–
Perhaps I will return immediately–
Do as I bid you, shut doors after you.
Fast bind, fast find,
A proverb never stale in thrifty mind.   [*Exit*

JESSICA   Farewell, and if my fortune be not crossed,
I have a father, you a daughter lost.   [*Exit*

Scene 6

Venice

Enter the masquers GRATIANO *and* SALERIO

GRATIANO   This is the penthouse under which Lorenzo
Desired us to make stand.

SALERIO   His hour is almost past.

GRATIANO   And it is marvel he out-dwells his hour,
For lovers ever run before the clock.

SALERIO   O ten times faster Venus' pigeons fly
To seal love's bonds new-made, than they are wont
To keep obliged faith unforfeited.

GRATIANO   That ever holds: who riseth from a feast
With that keen appetite that he sits down?
Where is the horse that doth untread again   10
His tedious measures with the unbated fire
That he did pace them first? All things that are,
Are with more spirit chased than enjoyed.
How like a younger or a prodigal
The scarfed bark puts from her native bay,
Hugged and embraced by the strumpet wind.
How like the prodigal doth she return,
With over-weathered ribs and ragged sails,
Lean, rent, and beggared by the strumpet wind.

Lorenzo arrives, and soon after Jessica appears, dressed as a boy, and throws down money she has taken from Shylock. She is alarmed at having to appear in public.

---

abode: delay

exchange: she has changed into boy's clothing to elope; she has exchanged Shylock for Lorenzo and she has turned into a thief – all for love

pretty: ingenious

hold...shames: shine a light on what I'm ashamed of

light: well-lit, obvious, and a play on words: light also meant immoral

office of discovery: revealing work. The job of a torch-bearer, hired for the evening, was to light his master through the dark and dirty streets.

garnish: outfit

close: secretive. Lorenzo says that night, which is hiding her away, is itself running out.

we are stayed for: they are expecting us

gild: supply

| SALERIO | Here comes Lorenzo, more of this hereafter. 20 |

Enter LORENZO

LORENZO	Sweet friends, your patience for my long abode.
	Not I, but my affairs, have made you wait.
	When you shall please to play the thieves for wives
	I'll watch as long for you then. Approach.
	Here dwells my father Jew. Ho, who's within?

Enter JESSICA *above, in boy's clothes*

| JESSICA | Who are you? Tell me for more certainty, |
| | Albeit I'll swear that I do know your tongue. |

| LORENZO | Lorenzo and thy love. |

JESSICA	Lorenzo certain, and my love indeed,
	For who love I so much? And now who knows 30
	But you Lorenzo, whether I am yours?

| LORENZO | Heaven and thy thoughts are witness that thou art. |

JESSICA	Here, catch this casket, it is worth the pains.
	I am glad 'tis night, you do not look on me,
	For I am much ashamed of my exchange.
	But love is blind, and lovers cannot see
	The pretty follies that themselves commit,
	For if they could, Cupid himself would blush
	To see me thus transformed to a boy.

| LORENZO | Descend, for you must be my torch-bearer. 40 |

JESSICA	What, must I hold a candle to my shames?
	They in themselves, good sooth, are too too light.
	Why, 'tis an office of discovery, love,
	And I should be obscured.

LORENZO	So are you, sweet,
	Even in the lovely garnish of a boy.
	But come at once,
	For the close night doth play the runaway,
	And we are stayed for at Bassanio's feast.

| JESSICA | I will make fast the doors, and gild myself |

Lorenzo speaks of his love for Jessica. She joins them and they go. Antonio has a message for Gratiano.

moe: more

1 Jessica goes inside to get more money. Lorenzo comments on his love for her; her wisdom, beauty and loyalty.
2 Lorenzo, Jessica and Salerio leave for the party.
3 Antonio rushes in looking for all those who are going to Belmont. The wind has changed and they must set sail at once. Gratiano is pleased.

ACTIVITIES

Keeping track

Scene 2

1 Why does Launcelot want to leave Shylock?
2 Why is Bassanio rather worried at the thought of taking Gratiano with him to Belmont?

With some moe ducats, and be with you straight. 50
[Exit above

GRATIANO   Now, by my hood, a gentle and no Jew.

LORENZO   Beshrew me but I love her heartily,
           For she is wise, if I can judge of her,
           And fair she is, if that mine eyes be true,
           And true she is, as she hath proved herself;
           And therefore like herself, wise, fair, and true,
           Shall she be placed in my constant soul.

           Enter JESSICA *below*

           What, art thou come? On gentlemen, away,
           Our masquing mates by this time for us stay.
[Exit with Jessica and Salerio

           Enter ANTONIO

ANTONIO   Who's there? 60

GRATIANO   Signior Antonio?

ANTONIO   Fie, fie Gratiano, where are all the rest?
           'Tis nine o'clock, our friends all stay for you.
           No masque tonight, the wind is come about;
           Bassanio presently will go aboard.
           I have sent twenty out to seek for you.

GRATIANO   I am glad on't, I desire no more delight.
           Than to be under sail, and gone tonight. [*Exeunt*

Scene 3

3 What does Jessica think of her life at home?
4 Which of Bassanio's friends is Jessica planning to marry?

Scene 4

5 How does Jessica get a message to her lover?
6 How will she be disguised for the elopement?

Scene 5

7 Why is Shylock uneasy about going out for the evening?

Scene 6

8 How does Launcelot manage to tell Jessica that Lorenzo will be there that evening?
9 What does Jessica throw down to Lorenzo?
10 Why is Antonio looking for Gratiano?

Discussion

1 In Act 2 scene 2, Launcelot is torn between what he knows he should do and what he wants to do. In pairs, discuss situations in which you find yourself in a similar predicament. For example:
  • You have left a lot of homework until the last moment. Unexpectedly there is a disco that evening.
  • You have promised to go with your younger brother or sister to the the dentist. The sales have just started and there is something you desperately want to buy.
  How do you decide what to do? Which would *you* do?
2 It is commonly accepted that parents have responsibilities to their children, but do children have responsibilities to their parents? What might these be?
3 In Act 2 scene 2, Launcelot deceives his father. In Act 2 scene 6, Jessica deceives hers. What does each of them hope to achieve? What are your opinions about their deceptions?
4 Why does Shylock tell Jessica to '*Lock up my doors*'?
5 Shylock is about to lose his daughter. What emotion do you feel? Do you feel sorry for him?

Drama

Comedy

When we study Shakespeare's plays in class we sometimes forget that they are meant to be acted, not read. In particular the comedy scenes suffer. Look at the antics of Launcelot and Gobbo in their anxiety to get Launcelot taken on as Bassanio's servant, in Act 2 scene 2 lines 114–142.

1 Some of the humour comes from the behaviour of the two clowns, with Launcelot constantly interrupting his father. What movement might be appropriate here?
2 Bassanio is the confused 'straight' man. How will he react?
3 Many words are used incorrectly, or are made up. How should these be emphasized?

Work in groups of four. Three of you play the three parts and the fourth direct the scene. Try to find ways of making your audience laugh.

Setting the scene

Work in pairs for this activity.

Many scenes in this section (Act 2 scenes 3, 4, 5, 6) are short. Many of them occur in different places and at different times of day. They are so short that it is unlikely that different sets would be provided for each scene.

• With a partner, work out how the changes of scene might be shown without moving scenery.
• You may find it useful to track the different characters and changes of scene using a diagram or flow chart.
• The changes should go smoothly so that the play flows quickly.
• You could present this as diagrams, pictures or a storyboard.

Character

1 Start CHARACTER LOGS (page 206) for Lorenzo and Jessica. Do you think you can rely on what they say about one another? It may be more helpful to look at how they behave, rather than at what they say, and make two columns headed 'positive' and 'negative' before you start the log.

2 Gratiano's request to accompany Bassanio to Belmont forces his friend to tell him some unpleasant truths (scene 2 lines 172–181). Start a CHARACTER LOG for Gratiano, referring back for earlier information to his speeches and the notes on Act 1 scene 1. Add to Bassanio's log.

Close study

Act 2 scene 5 lines 11–18 and 28–39

1 In both of these speeches Shylock is speaking to his daughter, Jessica. What is his attitude to her? What do you think her life is like?

2 What do Launcelot and the audience know, that Shylock does not know? (When the audience knows something that a character does not, the playwright is using *dramatic irony*, see GLOSSARY, page 234.

3 Even these words to his daughter are full of references to Shylock's hatred of Christians. Make a note of how he regards 'Christian' behaviour, and the words which express his distaste.

Act 2 scene 2 lines 114–142

Launcelot and his father are very anxious to find Launcelot a new job. They both want to impress Bassanio. Although Launcelot wants his father to speak for him, he sometimes feels he could do better himself. This leads to:

  a frequent interruptions
  b contradictions
  c misuse of words meant to impress.

1 Find examples of **a** and **b** and make a note of them.

2 Make a list of the words that are wrongly used and write alongside each what was really meant. (Start with '*infection*' and find three more.)

3 How different is Launcelot's style of speech when Bassanio asks, '*What would you?*'? Does this add to the comedy?

Writing

1 The director has asked you to make an authentic copy of the
   letter that Jessica asks Launcelot to deliver to Lorenzo.
   Individually, or in pairs:
   • Read Lorenzo's account of what the letter says (Act 2 scene
     4 lines 29–39).
   • Work out what the letter actually says. Lorenzo may have
     left some things out. What kind of things would he not
     want to report to Gratiano?
   • What should the letter look like?

2 Write a short extra scene after scene 6. Shylock goes to see a
   cousin of his, a middle-aged woman who has brought up a
   family. He wants advice. What sorts of worries and concerns do
   you think he will have about bringing up his daughter, who is
   now a young woman? What suggestions might his relation
   make?
   You might like to think about these points.
   • Does Jessica seem happy?
   • Does she run the house efficiently?
   • The city is a wicked place, full of temptations.
   • She doesn't get out enough.
   • She doesn't seem to have any friends of her own age.

Quiz

1 Name Old Gobbo's wife, and his horse.
2 Name two things Gratiano promises to do to prove he can
   behave properly.
3 At what time were Bassanio's guests expected to arrive?
4 Give three of Shylock's complaints about Launcelot.
5 Does Shylock like music?
Who says, and to whom:
6 '*Do I look like a cudgel?*'
7 '*I must go with you to Belmont.*'
8 '*I am provided of a torch-bearer.*'
9 '*I did dream of money-bags tonight.*'
10 '*I am much ashamed of my exchange.*'?

The Prince of Morocco comes to choose between the three caskets. He reads the inscriptions and starts to work out their inner meaning. He dismisses straightaway the idea of risking all for lead.

discover: reveal
several: different
all as: just as
hazard: risk
withal: as well
A golden...dross: a high-minded man is not attracted by what appears worthless
aught: anything
with her virgin hue: pure white in colour

Scene

Belmont

Flourish Cornets. Enter PORTIA *with the* PRINCE OF MOROCCO *and their trains*

PORTIA Go, draw aside the curtains, and discover
The several caskets to this noble prince.
Now make your choice.

MOROCCO The first of gold, who this inscription bears,
'Who chooseth me shall gain what many men
    desire'.
The second silver, which this promise carries,
'Who chooseth me shall get as much as he
    deserves'.
This third dull lead, with warning all as blunt,
'Who chooseth me must give and hazard all he
    hath'.
How shall I know if I do choose the right?   10

PORTIA The one of them contains my picture Prince:
If you choose that, then I am yours withal.

MOROCCO Some god direct my judgement. Let me see,
I will survey the inscriptions back again.
What says this leaden casket?
'Who chooseth me must give and hazard all he
    hath.'
Must give–for what? For lead? Hazard for lead?
This casket threatens. Men that hazard all
Do it in hope of fair advantages.
A golden mind stoops not to shows of dross,   20
I'll then nor give nor hazard aught for lead.
What says the silver with her virgin hue?
'Who chooseth me shall get as much as he
    deserves.'
As much as he deserves? Pause there Morocco,

He is tempted by the silver inscription because he is sure he deserves Portia, but thinking of her many suitors who desire her, he chooses gold.

---

with an even hand: fairly, equally

If thou...estimation: if you take the value you set on yourself

to be afeard...myself: to underestimate myself would just be a feeble undermining of my own value

In graces: in good looks

shrine: place of pilgrimage to relics of a saint

Hyrcanian deserts: a region of the ancient Persian Empire next to the Caspian Sea. It had the reputation of being very desolate and full of tigers and snakes.

vasty: vast, broad

The watery kingdom...heaven: the sea, whose mountainous waves challenge the sky

base: unworthy. Lead is a base metal, along with copper, zinc and tin, as opposed to the precious metals, gold, silver and platinum.

rib: enclose

cerecloth: a wax cloth used to wrap a corpse; a winding-sheet or shroud

immured: walled up

angel: a gold coin showing the archangel Michael piercing the dragon

insculped upon: engraved

And weigh thy value with an even hand.
If thou be'st rated by thy estimation,
Thou dost deserve enough, and yet enough
May not extend so far as to the lady.
And yet to be afeard of my deserving
Were but a weak disabling of myself.   30
As much as I deserve, why that's the lady.
I do in birth deserve her, and in fortunes,
In graces, and in qualities of breeding;
But more than these, in love I do deserve.
What if I strayed no further, but chose here?
Let's see once more this saying graved in gold:
'Who chooseth me shall gain what many men
    desire'.
Why that's the lady, all the world desires her.
From the four corners of the earth they come
To kiss this shrine, this mortal breathing saint.   40
The Hyrcanian deserts and the vasty wilds
Of wide Arabia are as throughfares now
For princes to come view fair Portia.
The watery kingdom, whose ambitious head
Spits in the face of heaven, is no bar
To stop the foreign spirits, but they come
As o'er a brook to see fair Portia.
One of these three contains her heavenly picture.
Is't like that lead contains her? 'Twere damnation
To think so base a thought; it were too gross   50
To rib her cerecloth in the obscure grave.
Or shall I think in silver she's immured,
Being ten times undervalued to tried gold?
O sinful thought, never so rich a gem
Was set in worse than gold. They have in England
A coin that bears the figure of an angel
Stamped in gold, but that's insculped upon;
But here an angel in a golden bed
Lies all within. Deliver me the key.
Here do I choose, and thrive I as I may.   60

Portia's portrait is not in the golden casket. The Prince has failed and leaves.

---

carrion Death: bony skull, death's head
But: just, merely
Gilded tombs...infold: tombs and monuments to the dead, which may be covered with gold on the outside will contain the horror of worms
inscrolled: written down in a scroll
suit is cold: courtship is over and done with
tedious: lengthy and formal
part: leave, go
A gentle riddance: a gentlemanly parting
complexion: temperament, disposition and colour

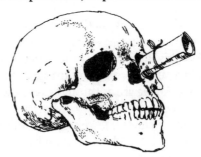

In Venice, Salerio and Solanio report Bassanio's departure and Shylock's anger.

PORTIA	There, take it Prince, and if my form lie there,
	Then I am yours.　　　[*He unlocks the golden casket*
MOROCCO	O hell! what have we here?

A carrion Death, within whose empty eye
There is a written scroll. I'll read the writing.

> 'All that glisters is not gold,
> Often have you heard that told.
> Many a man his life hath sold
> But my outside to behold.
> Gilded tombs do worms infold.
> Had you been as wise as bold,　　　　　　　　70
> Young in limbs, in judgement old,
> Your answer had not been inscrolled.
> Fare you well, your suit is cold.'

Cold indeed, and labour lost.
Then farewell heat, and welcome frost.
Portia adieu. I have too grieved a heart
To take a tedious leave. Thus losers part.
　　　　　　　　　　　　　　[*Exit with his train*

PORTIA	A gentle riddance. Draw the curtains, go.
	Let all of his complexion choose me so.　　[*Exeunt*

Scene 8

Venice

Enter SALERIO *and* SOLANIO

SALERIO	Why man, I saw Bassanio under sail,
	With him is Gratiano gone along;
	And in their ship I am sure Lorenzo is not.
SOLANIO	The villain Jew with outcries raised the duke,
	Who went with him to search Bassanio's ship.
SALERIO	He came too late, the ship was under sail.
	But there the duke was given to understand

Shylock has been seen in the streets lamenting the loss of his daughter and his ducats. There are fears that one of Antonio's ships has been wrecked.

certified: assured
Marry: indeed
reasoned: was talking
miscarried: was wrecked
richly fraught: with a valuable cargo
Slubber not: do not hurry over
stay...time: wait till the right moment
And for the Jew's...of love: as for the question of the bond I pledged to the Jew, do not let it concern you at all in your thoughts of love

That in a gondola were seen together
Lorenzo and his amorous Jessica.
Besides, Antonio certified the duke   10
They were not with Bassanio in his ship.

SOLANIO   I never heard a passion so confused,
So strange, outrageous, and so variable,
As the dog Jew did utter in the streets:
'My daughter! O my ducats! O my daughter!
Fled with a Christian! O my Christian ducats!
Justice! The law! My ducats, and my daughter!
A sealed bag, two sealed bags of ducats,
Of double ducats, stolen from me by my daughter,
And jewels, two stones, two rich and precious
        stones,   20
Stolen by my daughter. Justice! Find the girl!
She hath the stones upon her, and the ducats.'

SALERIO   Why, all the boys in Venice follow him,
Crying, his stones, his daughter, and his ducats.

SOLANIO   Let good Antonio look he keep his day
Or he shall pay for this.

SALERIO   Marry, well remembered.
I reasoned with a Frenchman yesterday,
Who told me, in the narrow seas that part
The French and English, there miscarried
A vessel of our country richly fraught.   30
I thought upon Antonio when he told me,
And wished in silence that it were not his.

SOLANIO   You were best to tell Antonio what you hear,
Yet do not suddenly, for it may grieve him.

SALERIO   A kinder gentleman treads not the earth.
I saw Bassanio and Antonio part,
Bassanio told him he would make some speed
Of his return. He answered, 'Do not so,
Slubber not business for my sake Bassanio,
But stay the very riping of the time;   40
And for the Jew's bond which he hath of me,

His friends report the emotional parting of Antonio from
Bassanio.

ostents: demonstrations
become you: be fitting for you
even there: at this point
affection wondrous sensible: with such deeply felt emotion
embraced heaviness: this melancholy mood he's taken on
Do we so: let's do that

In Belmont the Prince of Arragon is about to make his
choice of casket.

straight: straightaway
ta'en his oath: taken his oath (at the temple, as we are told in
    Act 2 scene 1 line 44)
election presently: choice immediately
nuptial rites: wedding ceremony
unfold: disclose

Let it not enter in your mind of love.
Be merry, and employ your chiefest thoughts
To courtship and such fair ostents of love
As shall conveniently become you there.'
And even there, his eye being big with tears,
Turning his face, he put his hand behind him,
And with affection wondrous sensible
He wrung Bassanio's hand; and so they parted.

SOLANIO   I think he only loves the world for him.   50
I pray thee let us go and find him out
And quicken his embraced heaviness
With some delight or other.

SALERIO   Do we so.   [*Exeunt*

Scene 9

Belmont

Enter NERISSA *and a Servant*

NERISSA   Quick, quick I pray thee, draw the curtain straight.
The Prince of Arragon hath ta'en his oath,
And comes to his election presently.

Flourish Cornets. Enter the PRINCE OF ARRAGON,
PORTIA, *and their trains*

PORTIA   Behold, there stand the caskets, noble prince.
If you choose that wherein I am contained,
Straight shall our nuptial rites be solemnized;
But if you fail, without more speech my lord,
You must be gone from hence immediately.

ARRAGON   I am enjoined by oath to observe three things:
First, never to unfold to any one   10
Which casket 'twas I chose; next, if I fail
Of the right casket, never in my life
To woo a maid in way of marriage; lastly,

Arragon immediately dismisses the idea of lead. He considers gold and then rejects it. He discusses silver and the concept of 'deserving'.

injunctions: (here) conditions
addressed me: prepared myself
ere: before
fond: foolish
pries not to: does not penetrate to
martlet: house-martin
in the...casualty: at risk and in danger of accident
jump: go along with
go about: make an effort
cozen: cheat
stamp: imprint
Without...merit?: Without really deserving it?
estates: status
degrees: social rank
offices: official positions
derived: acquired, obtained
cover: keep their hats on (as a sign of standing, or rank)
gleaned: picked out
how much...new-varnished?: Arragon is suggesting here that if people only rose through merit, and not through money or influence, then people pretending to be great would be weeded out and those deserving high office would be rescued from the poor conditions they had been forced into by the way society was organized.

If I do fail in fortune of my choice,
Immediately to leave you and be gone.

PORTIA   To these injunctions every one doth swear
That comes to hazard for my worthless self.

ARRAGON   And so have I addressed me—fortune now
To my heart's hope. Gold, silver, and base lead.
'Who chooseth me must give and hazard all he
    hath.'   20
You shall look fairer ere I give or hazard.
What says the golden chest? ha, let me see:
'Who chooseth me shall gain what many men
    desire'.
What many men desire—that 'many' may be meant
By the fool multitude that choose by show,
Not learning more than the fond eye doth teach,
Which pries not to the interior, but, like the martlet,
Builds in the weather on the outward wall,
Even in the force and road of casualty.
I will not choose what many men desire,   30
Because I will not jump with common spirits,
And rank me with the barbarous multitudes.
Why then to thee thou silver treasure-house,
Tell me once more what title thou dost bear:
'Who chooseth me shall get as much as he
    deserves'.
And well said too; for who shall go about
To cozen fortune and be honourable
Without the stamp of merit? Let none presume
To wear an undeserved dignity.
O that estates, degrees, and offices,   40
Were not derived corruptly, and that clear honour
Were purchased by the merit of the wearer.
How many then should cover that stand bare?
How many be commanded that command?
How much low peasantry would then be gleaned
From the true seed of honour, and how much
    honour

The Prince of Arragon assumes he deserves the best and chooses silver. He is not successful and leaves.

new-varnished: repainted, refurbished

I will assume desert: I will take it for granted that I do deserve Portia

blinking idiot: fool's head, picture of clown or jester

schedule: statement

To...natures: Portia points out that you can't be judge and defendant at the same time

tried: refined (as metals are heated to drive off impurities)

amiss: wrongly

I wis: certainly

Silvered o'er: with white hair (and so supposed to be wise)

I...head: whatever authority you may appear to have, you will always be a fool

sped: finished

ruth: calamity

Picked from the chaff and ruin of the times
To be new-varnished? Well, but to my choice.
'Who chooseth me shall get as much as he
    deserves.'
I will assume desert. Give me a key for this,   50
And instantly unlock my fortunes here.

                        [He opens the silver casket

PORTIA	Too long a pause for that which you find there.
ARRAGON	What's here? The portrait of a blinking idiot

Presenting me a schedule. I will read it.
How much unlike art thou to Portia.
How much unlike my hopes and my deservings.
'Who chooseth me shall have as much as he
    deserves.'
Did I deserve no more than a fool's head?
Is that my prize? Are my deserts no better?

PORTIA	To offend and judge are distinct offices 60
	And of opposed natures.
ARRAGON	What is here?

    'The fire seven times tried this:
    Seven times tried that judgement is,
    That did never choose amiss.
    Some there be that shadows kiss,
    Such have but a shadow's bliss.
    There be fools alive I wis,
    Silvered o'er; and so was this.
    Take what wife you will to bed,
    I will ever be your head.   70
    So be gone, you are sped.'
    Still more fool I shall appear
    By the time I linger here.
    With one fool's head I came to woo,
    But I go away with two.
    Sweet adieu. I'll keep my oath,
    Patiently to bear my ruth.

                        [Exeunt Arragon and train

No sooner has Arragon left than the approach of another suitor is announced. Could it be Bassanio?

---

deliberate fools: fools who spend their time deliberating, that is, considering their choice

They...lose: they have just enough sense to get things wrong when they use it

sensible regrets: substantial greetings (greetings backed up with gifts)

commends: compliments

breath: words

costly: lavish, rich

fore-spurrer: a horseman who rides ahead of the rest

high-day wit: excited turns of phrase

post: courier, messenger

mannerly: courteously

PORTIA	Thus hath the candle singed the moth.
	O these deliberate fools, when they do choose,
	They have the wisdom by their wit to lose. 80
NERISSA	The ancient saying is no heresy,
	Hanging and wiving goes by destiny.
PORTIA	Come draw the curtain Nerissa.

Enter a Servant

SERVANT	Where is my lady?
PORTIA	Here. What would my lord?
SERVANT	Madam, there is alighted at your gate
	A young Venetian, one that comes before
	To signify th'approaching of his lord;
	From whom he bringeth sensible regrets,
	To wit, besides commends and courteous breath,
	Gifts of rich value. Yet I have not seen 90
	So likely an ambassador of love.
	A day in April never came so sweet
	To show how costly summer was at hand,
	As this fore-spurrer comes before his lord.
PORTIA	No more I pray thee, I am half afeard
	Thou wilt say anon he is some kin to thee,
	Thou spend'st such high-day wit in praising him.
	Come, come Nerissa, for I long to see
	Quick Cupid's post that comes so mannerly.
NERISSA	Bassanio, Lord Love if thy will it be. [*Exeunt* 100

Antonio's friends say the rumour is still going round that one of his ships has been wrecked. They hope it is not true. Shylock, meeting them, accuses them of having known about Jessica's elopement.

it...unchecked: the rumour is still uncontradicted
the Goodwins: the Goodwin Sands, off the Kent coast, were notoriously dangerous to shipping
my gossip Report: my old friend Rumour. An example of personification (see GLOSSARY, page 236)
knapped: chewed, munched
without...prolixity: without slipping into wordiness
or crossing...talk: or abandoning plain speaking
Come, the full stop: bring it to an end

Act three

Scene 1

Venice

Enter SOLANIO *and* SALERIO

SOLANIO   Now what news on the Rialto?

SALERIO   Why yet it lives there unchecked, that Antonio hath
            a ship of rich lading wrecked on the narrow seas;
            the Goodwins I think they call the place, a very
            dangerous flat, and fatal, where the carcases of
            many a tall ship lie buried, as they say, if my gossip
            Report be an honest woman of her word.

SOLANIO   I would she were as lying a gossip in that as ever
            knapped ginger, or made her neighbours believe she
            wept for the death of a third husband. But it is   10
            true, without any slips of prolixity, or crossing the
            plain highway of talk, that the good Antonio, the
            honest Antonio–O that I had a title good enough
            to keep his name company–

SALERIO   Come, the full stop.

SOLANIO   Ha, what sayest thou? Why, the end is, he hath lost
            a ship.

SALERIO   I would it might prove the end of his losses.

SOLANIO   Let me say 'amen' betimes, lest the devil cross my
            prayer, for here he comes in the likeness of a Jew.   20

Enter SHYLOCK

            How now Shylock, what news among the
            merchants?

SHYLOCK   You knew, none so well, none so well as you, of my
            daughter's flight.

Shylock, while angry and hurt at Jessica's departure, makes it clear he will take revenge on Antonio if he defaults. He speaks passionately of Jews' and Christians' common humanity.

---

complexion: nature, temperament

dam: mother (bird). Shylock makes a play on the word when he uses '*damned*' in line 30.

My own flesh and blood: my child

Out upon it: expression of disgust

carrion: rotting flesh, carcass

rebels it...years: Solanio and Salerio are being deliberately unpleasant. They take Shylock's words to mean that 'even at his age' he has uncontrollable sexual urges.

rhenish: Rhine wine, a fine white wine

match: deal

smug: originally meant 'smart', 'neatly dressed'. At about the time Shakespeare was writing this play, the meaning was changing to include 'complacent'. Either or both meanings would fit well here.

mart: market, the exchange

hindered me: prevented my making

thwarted my bargains: spoiled my deals

dimensions: (human) proportions

SALERIO   That's certain. I for my part knew the tailor that
             made the wings she flew withal.

SOLANIO   And Shylock for his own part knew the bird was
             fledged, and then it is the complexion of them all to
             leave the dam.

SHYLOCK   She is damned for it.   30

SALERIO   That's certain, if the devil may be her judge.

SHYLOCK   My own flesh and blood to rebel.

SOLANIO   Out upon it old carrion, rebels it at these years?

SHYLOCK   I say my daughter is my flesh and blood.

SALERIO   There is more difference between thy flesh and hers,
             than between jet and ivory; more between your
             bloods, than there is between red wine and rhenish.
             But tell us, do you hear whether Antonio have had
             any loss at sea or no?

SHYLOCK   There I have another bad match, a bankrupt, a   40
             prodigal, who dare scarce show his head on the
             Rialto, a beggar, that was used to come so smug
             upon the mart. Let him look to his bond. He was
             wont to call me usurer, let him look to his bond.
             He was wont to lend money for a Christian
             courtesy, let him look to his bond.

SALERIO   Why I am sure, if he forfeit, thou wilt not take his
             flesh, what's that good for?

SHYLOCK   To bait fish withal. If it will feed nothing else, it will
             feed my revenge. He hath disgraced me, and   50
             hindered me half a million, laughed at my losses,
             mocked at my gains, scorned my nation, thwarted
             my bargains, cooled my friends, heated mine
             enemies, and what's his reason? I am a Jew. Hath
             not a Jew eyes? Hath not a Jew hands, organs,
             dimensions, senses, affections, passions? Fed with
             the same food, hurt with the same weapons, subject
             to the same diseases, healed by the same means,
             warmed and cooled by the same winter and

Shylock continues to insist on revenge. When Solanio and Salerio leave, Tubal reports to Shylock on his search for Jessica.

---

what is his humility?: the Christian teaching is to accept wrongs with humility. Shylock suggests that Christians do not practise what they preach, but want revenge.

sufferance: toleration, endurance

execute: carry out

it shall go...but: certainly

curse: see *Deuteronomy 28,* verses 15 onwards. This is a long list of curses afflicting every imaginable aspect of life, which God threatens will fall upon the Jews if they do not follow all his commandments.

hearsed: in her coffin

lights: settles

summer, as a Christian is? If you prick us do we   60
not bleed? If you tickle us do we not laugh? If you
poison us do we not die? And if you wrong us shall
we not revenge? If we are like you in the rest, we
will resemble you in that. If a Jew wrong a
Christian, what is his humility? Revenge. If a
Christian wrong a Jew, what should his sufferance
be by Christian example? Why revenge. The villany
you teach me I will execute, and it shall go hard but
I will better the instruction.

Enter a Servant

SERVANT   Gentlemen, my master Antonio is at his house,   70
and desires to speak with you both.

SALERIO   We have been up and down to seek him.

Enter TUBAL

SOLANIO   Here comes another of the tribe; a third cannot be
matched, unless the devil himself turn Jew.
                      [Exeunt Solanio, Salerio, and Servant

SHYLOCK   How now Tubal, what news from Genoa? Hast
thou found my daughter?

TUBAL   I often came where I did hear of her, but cannot
find her.

SHYLOCK   Why there, there, there, there, a diamond gone cost
me two thousand ducats in Frankfort. The curse   80
never fell upon our nation till now, I never felt it till
now. Two thousand ducats in that, and other
precious, precious jewels. I would my daughter
were dead at my foot, and the jewels in her ear.
Would she were hearsed at my foot, and the ducats
in her coffin. No news of them? Why so–and I
know not what's spent in the search. Why thou loss
upon loss. The thief gone with so much, and so
much to find the thief, and no satisfaction, no
revenge, nor no ill luck stirring but what lights   90

Tubal has heard of the loss of a second ship of Antonio's.
He also tells of Jessica's spending spree. Shylock starts to
make arrangements for the forfeit of Antonio's bond.

cast away: wrecked
divers of Antonio's creditors: several men to whom Antonio
    owes money
break: fail, go bankrupt
Leah: presumably Shylock's wife, now dead
fee me an officer: pay for an arresting officer for me
bespeak him: book him, engage him
were he...I will: if he were removed from Venice I could make
    whatever deals I chose

	on my shoulders, no sighs but of my breathing, no tears but of my shedding.
TUBAL	Yes, other men have ill luck too. Antonio, as I heard in Genoa–
SHYLOCK	What, what, what? Ill luck, ill luck?
TUBAL	Hath an argosy cast away coming from Tripolis.
SHYLOCK	I thank God, I thank God. Is it true, is it true?
TUBAL	I spoke with some of the sailors that escaped the wreck.
SHYLOCK	I thank thee good Tubal, good news, good 100 news! Ha, ha! Heard in Genoa?
TUBAL	Your daughter spent in Genoa, as I heard, one night fourscore ducats.
SHYLOCK	Thou stick'st a dagger in me. I shall never see my gold again. Fourscore ducats at a sitting, fourscore ducats.
TUBAL	There came divers of Antonio's creditors in my company to Venice, that swear he cannot choose but break.
SHYLOCK	I am very glad of it, I'll plague him, I'll torture 110 him. I am glad of it.
TUBAL	One of them showed me a ring that he had of your daughter for a monkey.
SHYLOCK	Out upon her, thou torturest me Tubal. It was my turquoise, I had it of Leah when I was a bachelor. I would not have given it for a wilderness of monkeys.
TUBAL	But Antonio is certainly undone.
SHYLOCK	Nay, that's true, that's very true. Go Tubal, fee me an officer; bespeak him a fortnight before. I 120 will have the heart of him if he forfeit, for were he out of Venice, I can make what merchandise I will. Go Tubal, and meet me at our synagogue. Go good Tubal, at our synagogue Tubal. [*Exeunt*

 CTIVITIES

Keeping track

Act 2 scene 7

1 According to the Prince of Morocco, which is the only casket worthy to contain Portia's portrait?

Act 2 scene 8

2 What double disaster has struck Shylock?
3 Where did Shylock think Lorenzo and Jessica might be?
4 How did Bassanio and Antonio part?
5 What is the first suggestion of trouble for Antonio?

Act 2 scene 9

6 What is the purpose of the rhymes in the caskets?

Act 3 scene 1

7 Why does Shylock assume that Solanio and Salerio know of Jessica's flight?
8 In Act 3 scene 1 there is a second suggestion of misfortune for Antonio. What is it?
9 Who has been looking for Lorenzo and Jessica?
10 Where do Shylock and Tubal arrange to meet?

Discussion

1 Write down the three conditions which the suitors must agree to. What is the purpose of these? From evidence in the play so far, does the intention seem to work? Do you think Portia knows what is in each casket at the beginning?
2 What do you think Portia will be feeling in Act 2 scene 7:
   • at the beginning
   • while Morocco is making his choice
   • at the end?

3 What is the Prince of Morocco's opinion: of himself, and of Portia?

4 What does the Prince base his choice on?

5 In Act 2 scene 9, the Prince of Arragon discards the golden casket. Why? What does his interpretation of the inscription tell us about his character?

6 What was Portia's father trying to achieve by the use of the caskets?

7 What is Portia's reaction to the news of Bassanio's arrival?

8 In Act 3 scene 1, Shylock's first words give the impression of a man pushed beyond the limits. In Act 2 scene 8, Salerio and Solanio have shown that they have no sympathy for him. They still call him '*villain*', '*dog*', and '*devil*'.
   - How do you feel about Shylock's double loss? Suggest lines which show: his hurt, his rage, his complete loneliness.
   - Do you think he cares more about losing the ducats or his daughter? Which loss does he mention first?
   - Shylock is powerless to get back his daughter or his money. Antonio is in *his* power. Find his first mention of revenge.
   - In Act 3 scene 1 lines 54–62, Shylock says that Jews are people too, and that they are made of the same stuff as Christians. Do you find sympathy for him here?
   - This scene has been described as the turning-point of the play. Do you agree?

Drama

1 We see the Prince of Morocco and the Prince of Arragon only in their role as suitors for Portia. Any actors cast as these two men would need to invent a history for their character to prevent their portrayal being superficial.
   - Work in a group of six or seven.
   - Decide whether you will investigate Arragon or Morocco.
   - Choose two investigators in your group and cast the rest of the group as people to be interviewed. For example:
     army officers – soldiers' wives – personal servants – cooks
     prisoners-of-war – barbers – ex-tutors – parents…

- Jot down a list of the things you want to know about them based on how they appear in the play – for example: why are they so proud?
- Carry out the interviews.

Present your reports verbally to your teacher, who represents Portia. The rest of the class, Portia's advisers, should comment on whether the reports fit what they know of the characters in the play.

2 Imagine that Solanio and Salerio report their conversation with Shylock to the press.
  - Work in groups of four. Two are Solanio and Salerio. Two are newspaper reporters who want a good story.
  - Carry out the interviews. (There could be a variety of newspapers, local and national, daily and weekly, including *The Jewish Herald*.)
  - Produce the copy (the words).
  - The reporters can take turns to read it out to the class, as though they were ringing it through to the office.

Character

1 What do you think Portia means by her remark after the Prince of Morocco's departure? What does it tell you about her character? How do you think an actress should deliver these lines?

2 What functions do Solanio and Salerio perform in Act 2 scene 8 and in Act 3 scene 1? You will be helped in your answer if you think about how you would want to deal with these scenes if you were making a film of the play.

3 Scene 8 also gives you some evidence of the relationship between Bassanio and Antonio. Add to their CHARACTER LOGS.

4 Re-read Act 3 scene 1 carefully and add your findings to Shylock's CHARACTER LOG.

Close study

Scene 7 lines 65–73

Much of the play is written in blank verse (see page 212), but scenes written in blank verse often end with a rhyming couplet. Suddenly there is a verse of nine shorter lines, all rhyming with 'gold'.

1 What effect do you think this insistent rhyme is meant to have on the Prince of Morocco, who has just failed to win Portia? What do you notice about the way he and Portia speak after hearing the rhymes?
2 There is a similar, ten-line verse in the silver casket. Do all these lines have the same rhyme? How does the Prince of Arragon speak after reading his verse?
3 What is the last line of each 'poem' reserved for?
4 Can you find any rhymes in the rest of the scene?
5 What does this passage show you about Shakespeare's use of rhyme?

Writing

1 One of the Prince of Morocco's servants has been left behind to look after a lame horse. He is in the servants' hall when the Prince of Arragon's servants arrive. Write the conversation he has with one of the new arrivals. Perhaps one of Portia's servants joins in.
2 Imagine that you are Tubal. Write a diary entry in which you consider Shylock's behaviour. Do you agree with him, sympathize, understand? Or are you shocked and disturbed?

Quiz

1 What is in the gold casket?
2 To whom did Venetians take their problems when something went seriously wrong?
3 What is in the silver casket?
4 How much money did Jessica spend in one evening?
5 What did she buy with a ring?
6 What stone was set in this ring?
7 Name the places where two of Antonio's ships are reported wrecked.

Portia, in danger of giving away her feelings for Bassanio, asks him to delay choosing. He cannot bear to wait.

---

tarry: delay

forbear: withdraw

in such a quality: in such a manner

lest: in case

And yet...thought: a girl is not supposed to speak her thoughts on the subject of love

I am then forsworn: if I did that I would have broken my oath (her solemn promise to her dying father)

But if...forsworn: Portia says that if Bassanio fails to make the right choice, he'll make her wish she'd committed a sin – that she had broken her oath and told him how to choose.

Beshrew: a mild or jokey curse

o'erlooked: bewitched

naughty: wicked

peize: weigh down

eke: make it last

election: choice

rack: the medieval instrument of torture. It was used to extract confessions particularly from people held for treason. In the following fourteen lines Portia and Bassanio play with the ideas of forced confession, of mistrust and of loyalty. They confess their love for one another.

Scene 2

Belmont

Enter BASSANIO, PORTIA, GRATIANO, NERISSA, *and Attendants*

PORTIA   I pray you tarry, pause a day or two
Before you hazard, for in choosing wrong
I lose your company; therefore forbear awhile.
There's something tells me–but it is not love–
I would not lose you, and you know yourself
Hate counsels not in such a quality.
But lest you should not understand me well–
And yet a maiden hath no tongue but thought–
I would detain you here some month or two
Before you venture for me. I could teach you   10
How to choose right, but I am then forsworn;
So will I never be, so may you miss me;
But if you do, you'll make me wish a sin,
That I had been forsworn. Beshrew your eyes,
They have o'erlooked me, and divided me;
One half of me is yours, the other half yours–
Mine own I would say, but if mine then yours,
And so all yours. O these naughty times
Put bars between the owners and their rights.
And so though yours, not yours. Prove it so.   20
Let fortune go to hell for it, not I.
I speak too long, but 'tis to peize the time,
To eke it, and to draw it out in length,
To stay you from election.

BASSANIO   Let me choose,
For as I am, I live upon the rack.

PORTIA   Upon the rack Bassanio then confess
What treason there is mingled with your love.

BASSANIO   None but that ugly treason of mistrust,

Portia orders music while Bassanio makes his choice: it will be a swan-song if he fails, a fanfare if he wins her.

amity: friendship

Had been the very sum: would have been the total amount

Doth teach me...deliverance: teaches me the answers I should give to make the torture stop

all aloof: some distance away

a swan-like end: the ancient belief was that a swan would sing just before its death

flourish: fanfare

dulcet: sweet

Alcides: one of the names for Hercules or Herakles (he was the grandson of Alcaeus). Lines 53–61 refer to a story about him: the King of Troy, Laomedon, had his daughter Hesione chained to a rock. She was to be torn apart and devoured by a sea monster as an offering to the gods he had offended. Hercules rescued her, and killed the monster, not for love, but for the promised reward of six fine horses – which he did not receive.

virgin tribute: sacrifice of Hesione, daughter of the King of Troy

Dardanian wives: Trojan women

bleared: tear-stained

issue: result

fray: fight

	Which makes me fear the enjoying of my love.	
	There may as well be amity and life	30
	'Tween snow and fire, as treason and my love.	
PORTIA	Ay but I fear you speak upon the rack	
	Where men enforced do speak anything.	
BASSANIO	Promise me life, and I'll confess the truth.	
PORTIA	Well then, confess and live.	
BASSANIO	'Confess' and 'love'	

Had been the very sum of my confession.
O happy torment, when my torturer
Doth teach me answers for deliverance.
But let me to my fortune and the caskets.

PORTIA   Away then, I am locked in one of them,   40
If you do love me, you will find me out.
Nerissa and the rest, stand all aloof,
Let music sound while he doth make his choice;
Then if he lose he makes a swan-like end,
Fading in music. That the comparison
May stand more proper, my eye shall be the stream
And watery death-bed for him. He may win,
And what is music then? Then music is
Even as the flourish, when true subjects bow
To a new-crowned monarch. Such it is   50
As are those dulcet sounds in break of day
That creep into the dreaming bridegroom's ear
And summon him to marriage. Now he goes
With no less presence, but with much more love,
Than young Alcides, when he did redeem
The virgin tribute paid by howling Troy
To the sea-monster. I stand for sacrifice;
The rest aloof are the Dardanian wives,
With bleared visages come forth to view
The issue of th'exploit. Go Hercules.   60
Live thou, I live. With much much more dismay
I view the fight than thou that mak'st the fray.

While the song is being sung, Bassanio expresses his thoughts on areas of life where the external appearance can hide something much less attractive: the law, religion, bravery, beauty.

comments...to himself: considers the inscriptions silently

fancy: love, attraction

begot: created

It is engendered: it comes into being. The song suggests that if love is only based on sight, on the outward show, it will not last very long.

still: continually

tainted: contaminated. The metaphor is of tainted food, particularly meat which, when it was going off, needed seasoning or spices to mask the bad flavour.

sober brow: serious person

approve it: demonstrate it to be true

livers...milk: without red blood and so white, cowardly

these: these men

valour's excrement: beards, an outward show of bravery

redoubted: feared

purchased...weight: cosmetics were bought by weight. The '*miracle*' which Bassanio speaks of, is that those women who wear most (weight of) make-up are also the '*lightest*'. The play on words here is that 'light' also means 'frivolous' or 'immoral'.

crisped: curled

Which...wind: which play so lovingly with the wind

Upon supposed fairness: pretending beauty

dowry: money and goods which a bride brought to her husband. Here used in the sense of 'legacy'.

The skull...sepulchre: the head on which the hair had grown, now a skull in the tomb. Hair was sold to be made into wigs.

A song to music the whilst BASSANIO *comments on the caskets to himself*

> Tell me where is fancy bred,
> Or in the heart or in the head?
> How begot, how nourished?

ALL   Reply, reply.
> It is engendered in the eyes,
> With gazing fed; and fancy dies
> In the cradle where it lies.
> > Let us all ring fancy's knell;   70
> > I'll begin it, ding, dong, bell.

ALL   Ding, dong, bell.

BASSANIO   So may the outward shows be least themselves.
The world is still deceived with ornament.
In law, what plea so tainted and corrupt
But being seasoned with a gracious voice,
Obscures the show of evil? In religion,
What damned error but some sober brow
Will bless it, and approve it with a text,
Hiding the grossness with fair ornament?   80
There is no vice so simple, but assumes
Some mark of virtue on his outward parts.
How many cowards whose hearts are all as false
As stairs of sand, wear yet upon their chins
The beards of Hercules and frowning Mars,
Who inward searched, have livers white as milk?
And these assume but valour's excrement
To render them redoubted. Look on beauty,
And you shall see 'tis purchased by the weight,
Which therein works a miracle in nature,   90
Making them lightest that wear most of it.
So are those crisped snaky golden locks
Which make such wanton gambols with the wind
Upon supposed fairness, often known
To be the dowry of a second head,
The skull that bred them in the sepulchre.

As a result of his deliberations Bassanio chooses the least
showy casket – lead. Portia and Bassanio are delighted
that he has chosen the correct casket.

---

guiled: treacherous
Veiling…beauty: Elizabethan fashion demanded fair, not dark,
  beauty
seeming: apparent
Hard food for Midas: King Midas, given one wish as a reward
  by Dionysus, asked that everything he touched be turned to
  gold. He soon found he couldn't eat gold.
palled: over-used, boring
common drudge: everyone's servant. Silver was used for coins,
  and so served everyone.
fleet to air: evaporate
As: such as
rash-embraced: too quickly adopted
jealousy: mistrust
allay: reduce
measure: moderation
rain: pour
scant: tone down
counterfeit: portrait
Or…motion: Or is it because my eyes are looking at them,
  they seem to move?
severed: parted
sunder: part
mesh: web
Faster: more securely
Having…unfurnished: once he had painted one of her eyes so
  beautifully the painter would only be able to gaze at it and
  so be unable to paint the other one
substance: wealth
Yet…substance: see to what extent the wealth of my praise
  does not do justice to the picture because it undervalues it;
  to the same extent the picture is nowhere near the original
  (Portia herself)
continent: store

Thus ornament is but the guiled shore
To a most dangerous sea, the beauteous scarf
Veiling an Indian beauty; in a word,
The seeming truth which cunning times put on   100
To entrap the wisest. Therefore thou gaudy gold,
Hard food for Midas, I will none of thee.
Nor none of thee, thou palled and common drudge
'Tween man and man. But thou, thou meagre lead
Which rather threatenest than dost promise aught,
Thy paleness moves me more than eloquence,
And here choose I, joy be the consequence.

PORTIA   [*Aside*] How all the other passions fleet to air,
As doubtful thoughts, and rash-embraced despair,
And shuddering fear, and green-eyed jealousy.   110
O love be moderate, allay thy ecstasy,
In measure rain thy joy, scant this excess.
I feel too much thy blessing, make it less
For fear I surfeit.

BASSANIO   What find I here?
                                   [*He opens the leaden casket*
Fair Portia's counterfeit. What demi-god
Hath come so near creation? Move these eyes?
Or whether riding on the balls of mine
Seem they in motion? Here are severed lips
Parted with sugar breath, so sweet a bar
Should sunder such sweet friends. Here in her
          hairs   120
The painter plays the spider, and hath woven
A golden mesh t'entrap the hearts of men
Faster than gnats in cobwebs: but her eyes–
How could he see to do them? Having made one,
Methinks it should have power to steal both his
And leave itself unfurnished. Yet look how far
The substance of my praise doth wrong this shadow
In underprizing it, so far this shadow
Doth limp behind the substance. Here's the scroll,
The continent and summary of my fortune.   130

Bassanio reads his scroll and turns to Portia to claim his kiss. She happily offers all she is, and has, to him.

---

by note: by this account. '*Note*' is both a bill, and a reference to the scroll.

Like one...ratified by you: Bassanio compares himself to someone competing with one other in a sport. He hears the applause and thinks he has won, but he can't be sure until he is told it is so.

account: opinion

livings: possessions

account: reckoning, counting up

term in gross: give in full

But now: a moment ago

'You that choose not by the view,
Chance as fair and choose as true.
Since this fortune falls to you,
Be content and seek no new.
If you be well pleased with this
And hold your fortune for your bliss,
Turn you where your lady is,
And claim her with a loving kiss.'

A gentle scroll. Fair lady, by your leave.
I come by note to give, and to receive.   140
Like one of two contending in a prize
That thinks he hath done well in people's eyes,
Hearing applause and universal shout,
Giddy in spirit, still gazing in a doubt
Whether those peals of praise be his or no,
So thrice-fair lady stand I even so,
As doubtful whether what I see be true,
Until confirmed, signed, ratified by you.

PORTIA   You see me Lord Bassanio where I stand,
Such as I am. Though for myself alone   150
I would not be ambitious in my wish,
To wish myself much better, yet for you,
I would be trebled twenty times myself,
A thousand times more fair, ten thousand times
More rich, that only to stand high in your account,
I might in virtues, beauties, livings, friends,
Exceed account. But the full sum of me
Is sum of nothing; which to term in gross,
Is an unlessoned girl, unschooled, unpractised,
Happy in this, she is not yet so old   160
But she may learn; happier than this,
She is not bred so dull but she can learn;
Happiest of all, is that her gentle spirit
Commits itself to yours to be directed,
As from her lord, her governor, her king.
Myself, and what is mine, to you and yours
Is now converted. But now I was the lord
Of this fair mansion, master of my servants,

Portia gives Bassanio a ring to confirm that they will
marry. He is never to part with it. Nerissa and Gratiano
congratulate them: they, too, wish to marry.

---

even now, but now: from this very moment
presage: foretell
vantage: opportunity
exclaim on: protest to, reproach
bereft me: robbed me
blent: blended
wild of nothing: a confused din

1 Gratiano joins Nerissa in wishing Portia and Bassanio joy,
   and then asks if he may marry at the same time.
2 Gratiano has fallen in love with Nerissa.

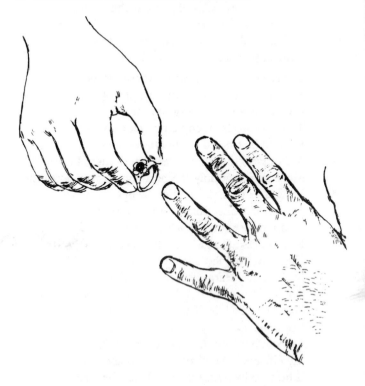

	Queen o'er myself. And even now, but now,
	This house, these servants and this same myself 170
	Are yours–my lord's–I give them with this ring,
	Which when you part from, lose, or give away,
	Let it presage the ruin of your love,
	And be my vantage to exclaim on you.
BASSANIO	Madam, you have bereft me of all words,
	Only my blood speaks to you in my veins,
	And there is such confusion in my powers,
	As after some oration fairly spoke
	By a beloved prince, there doth appear
	Among the buzzing pleased multitude, 180
	Where every something, being blent together,
	Turns to a wild of nothing, save of joy
	Expressed, and not expressed. But when this ring
	Parts from this finger, then parts life from hence:
	O then be bold to say Bassanio's dead.
NERISSA	My lord and lady, it is now our time
	That have stood by and seen our wishes prosper,
	To cry 'good joy', good joy my lord and lady.
GRATIANO	My lord Bassanio and my gentle lady,
	I wish you all the joy that you can wish, 190
	For I am sure you can wish none from me.
	And when your honours mean to solemnize
	The bargain of your faith, I do beseech you
	Even at that time I may be married too.
BASSANIO	With all my heart, so thou canst get a wife.
GRATIANO	I thank your lordship, you have got me one.
	My eyes my lord can look as swift as yours.
	You saw the mistress, I beheld the maid.
	You loved, I loved, for intermission
	No more pertains to me my lord than you. 200
	Your fortune stood upon the casket there,
	And so did mine too as the matter falls.
	For wooing here until I sweat again,
	And swearing till my very roof was dry

The double wedding is promised. Visitors arrive from Venice.

3 〉

3 Just as Bassanio's luck depended on his choice of casket, so did Gratiano's.

4 〉

4 Nerissa had agreed to marry Gratiano if Bassanio was successful. They will share Portia's and Bassanio's wedding. Gratiano wants to bet on who first produces a son.

5 〉

5 Lorenzo and Jessica arrive from Venice with Salerio.

6 〉

6 Salerio brings a letter for Bassanio from Antonio.

	With oaths of love, at last, if promise last,
	I got a promise of this fair one here
	To have her love, provided that your fortune
	Achieved her mistress.
PORTIA	Is this true Nerissa?
NERISSA	Madam it is, so you stand pleased withal.
BASSANIO	And do you Gratiano mean good faith? 210
GRATIANO	Yes faith, my lord.
BASSANIO	Our feast shall be much honoured in your marriage.
GRATIANO	We'll play with them the first boy for a thousand ducats.
NERISSA	What, and stake down?
GRATIANO	No, we shall ne'er win at that sport, and stake down.
BASSANIO	But who comes here? Lorenzo and his infidel? What, and my old Venetian friend Salerio?

Enter LORENZO, JESSICA, *and* SALERIO, *a Messenger from Venice*

BASSANIO	Lorenzo and Salerio, welcome hither, 220
	If that the youth of my new interest here
	Have power to bid you welcome. By your leave,
	I bid my very friends and countrymen,
	Sweet Portia, welcome,
PORTIA	So do I my lord,
	They are entirely welcome.
LORENZO	I thank your honour. For my part my lord,
	My purpose was not to have seen you here,
	But meeting with Salerio by the way
	He did intreat me past all saying nay
	To come with him along.
SALERIO	I did my lord, 230
	And I have reason for it. Signior Antonio
	Commends him to you. [*Gives Bassanio a letter*

Gratiano's mood does not fit with the news of Antonio. As Bassanio starts to read the letter Portia perceives that it contains really bad news. Bassanio admits the sad state of his affairs and his debt to Antonio.

7

7 Salerio makes it plain the letter contains bad news.

cheer: greet
yond stranger: that visitor (Jessica)
We are the Jasons...lost: Gratiano, with his usual lack of sensitivity, boasts of their success. With a punning reference to '*fleece*'/'*fleets*', Salerio points up Antonio's disastrous situation.
shrewd contents: bad news. '*Shrewd*' meant 'evil'.
turn...man: so affect the mood of a balanced man
blotted: stained
How...braggart: how boastful I was being
state: estate, property
engaged: bound, pledged
mere: absolute
feed my means: supply me with money

BASSANIO	Ere I ope his letter
	I pray you tell me how my good friend doth.
SALERIO	Not sick my lord, unless it be in mind,
	Nor well, unless in mind. His letter there
	Will show you his estate. *[Bassanio opens the letter*
GRATIANO	Nerissa, cheer yond stranger, bid her welcome.
	Your hand Salerio, what's the news from Venice?
	How doth that royal merchant, good Antonio?
	I know he will be glad of our success.
	We are the Jasons, we have won the fleece.
SALERIO	I would you had won the fleece that he hath lost.
PORTIA	There are some shrewd contents in yond same paper
	That steals the colour from Bassanio's cheek.
	Some dear friend dead, else nothing in the world
	Could turn so much the constitution
	Of any constant man. What, worse and worse?
	With leave Bassanio, I am half yourself,
	And I must freely have the half of anything
	That this same paper brings you.
BASSANIO	O sweet Portia,
	Here are a few of the unpleasant'st words
	That ever blotted paper. Gentle lady,
	When I did first impart my love to you,
	I freely told you all the wealth I had
	Ran in my veins–I was a gentleman,
	And then I told you true. And yet dear lady,
	Rating myself at nothing, you shall see
	How much I was a braggart. When I told you
	My state was nothing, I should then have told
	you
	That I was worse than nothing; for indeed
	I have engaged myself to a dear friend,
	Engaged my friend to his mere enemy
	To feed my means. Here is a letter lady;
	The paper as the body of my friend,
	And every word in it a gaping wound

Line numbers in right margin: 240 (at "I know he will be glad of our success."), 250 (at "O sweet Portia,"), 260 (at "That I was worse than nothing; for indeed").

The letter tells that Antonio's ships are all wrecked. Shylock is demanding his bond and would not accept money even if it were available. Bassanio praises Antonio.

Issuing life-blood: with his life bleeding away
hit: succeeded
Barbary: the North African coast
merchant-marring: ship-breaking
present money: ready money
discharge: pay off
keen: sharp
confound: destroy
plies: appeals to, petitions
impeach...justice: accuse the state of not holding to its own laws if he is denied justice
magnificoes: chief citizens of Venice
port: status
envious: malicious
The best-conditioned: with the best qualities
unwearied spirit...courtesies: never tired of doing kindnesses

Issuing life-blood. But is it true Salerio?
Have all his ventures failed? What not one hit?
From Tripolis, from Mexico and England,
From Lisbon, Barbary and India?
And not one vessel 'scape the dreadful touch   270
Of merchant-marring rocks?

SALERIO   Not one my lord.
Besides, it should appear, that if he had
The present money to discharge the Jew,
He would not take it. Never did I know
A creature that did bear the shape of man
So keen and greedy to confound a man.
He plies the duke at morning and at night,
And doth impeach the freedom of the state
If they deny him justice. Twenty merchants,
The duke himself, and the magnificoes   280
Of greatest port have all persuaded with him,
But none can drive him from the envious plea
Of forfeiture, of justice, and his bond.

JESSICA   When I was with him, I have heard him swear
To Tubal and to Chus, his countrymen,
That he would rather have Antonio's flesh
Than twenty times the value of the sum
That he did owe him. And I know my lord,
If law, authority, and power deny not,
It will go hard with poor Antonio.   290

PORTIA   Is it your dear friend that is thus in trouble?

BASSANIO   The dearest friend to me, the kindest man,
The best-conditioned and unwearied spirit
In doing courtesies; and one in whom
The ancient Roman honour more appears
Than any that draws breath in Italy.

PORTIA   What sum owes he the Jew?

Portia offers any amount of money to save Bassanio's friend. They shall marry straightaway but then Bassanio must go direct to Venice.

---

deface: cancel
unquiet: anxious
a merry cheer: a cheerful face
dispatch: settle
No bed...twain: Bassanio will not let either sleep or rest come between him and Portia till his return

BASSANIO	For me three thousand ducats.

PORTIA   What, no more?
Pay him six thousand, and deface the bond;
Double six thousand, and then treble that,   300
Before a friend of this description
Shall lose a hair through Bassanio's fault.
First go with me to church, and call me wife,
And then away to Venice to your friend.
For never shall you lie by Portia's side
With an unquiet soul. You shall have gold
To pay the petty debt twenty times over.
When it is paid, bring your true friend along.
My maid Nerissa and myself meantime
Will live as maids and widows. Come away   310
For you shall hence upon your wedding-day.
Bid your friends welcome, show a merry cheer,
Since you are dear bought, I will love you dear.
But let me hear the letter of your friend.

BASSANIO   [*Reads*] Sweet Bassanio, my ships have all
miscarried, my creditors grow cruel, my estate is
very low, my bond to the Jew is forfeit, and since in
paying it, it is impossible I should live, all debts are
cleared between you and I if I might but see
you at my death. Notwithstanding, use your   320
pleasure; if your love do not persuade you to come,
let not my letter.

PORTIA   O love, dispatch all business and be gone.

BASSANIO   Since I have your good leave to go away,
        I will make haste; but till I come again,
No bed shall e'er be guilty of my stay,
        Nor rest be interposer 'twixt us twain.   [*Exeunt*

CTIVITIES

Keeping track

1 Why does Portia want Bassanio to delay his choice?
2 What makes Bassanio choose lead?
3 What did Gratiano's and Nerissa's wish to marry depend on?
4 How does Portia know that the letter contains bad news?
5 What help does Portia offer straightaway?
6 Why do we not expect this help to be successful?

Discussion

1 What are Bassanio's reasons for discarding the gold and silver caskets?
2 What does Portia's speech, scene 2 lines 166–174 reveal about the expected role of a woman in marriage?
3 In appearing at Belmont with all the trappings of wealth, and with servants in smart new liveries, Bassanio has been acting a lie. Not only is he not rich, he is seriously in debt. Do you think that Portia would still have loved him had she realized this before?

Drama

1 In Portia's speech, Act 3 scene 2 lines 149–174, she surrenders herself to Bassanio, who has 'won' her. Some actresses may well have trouble with the sentiments Portia has to express here.
   Group work
   • Divide the speech into sections about five lines long.
   • Work in groups of five or six.
   • One member of the group represents a strong actress who has to say this speech but would rather cut it all, because it makes her seem weak.

- The rest of the group must convince her to keep the speech and say it in a way that satisfies her.
- Now take one of the sections of the speech and decide how it should be prepared.
- Should it be ironic, or sarcastic?
- Does she really love him?
- Is she really going to give up all her power?

Class work

Bring the whole speech together, with different Portias reading the parts they have worked on to produce a powerful version.

2 In scene 2 lines 279–283, Salerio talks of the numerous attempts to dissuade Shylock from his proposed course of action.

Preparation

- Spend some time in groups of two or three, considering what persuasive arguments they might use.
- Should they use arguments or threats?
- How does Shylock respond?
- Does he ignore them or answer back?

Hotseating (see page 208)

Either set this up as an ordinary 'hotseating' session with Shylock in the circle of questioners, or create a scene where Shylock moves across the Rialto bridge, accosted by small groups of questioners as he passses.

Character

1 In the previous scenes where we have seen Portia, she has been in control of the situation, so she has been able to appear detached and amused. What is different about her at the beginning of scene 2?

2 What do you notice about Bassanio's behaviour in lines 220–224 and 256–263? How would you describe these aspects of his character?

3 What is Portia's attitude to friendship?

4 How does Bassanio respond when, perhaps for the first time, he has to make a sacrifice in his friendship with Antonio?

Close study

1 Look at Portia's first speech in scene 2. The writing shows her agitation.
   - Find lines where her train of thought suddenly changes, or is interrupted by another consideration.
   - How many lines are punctuated in the middle in some way, to help demonstrate this?
   - Find the lines where she considers the idea of telling Bassanio the answer. Why doesn't she? How does the repetition of '*forsworn*' show how her mind is working?
   - Compared with her usual calm and clever delivery, she is almost gabbling. Which line tells us that she realizes this, and the reason for it?
2 Some commentators suggest that the choice of rhymes in scene 2 lines 63–65 is to tell Bassanio how to choose, because they rhyme with 'lead'. Considering what you have learnt from her first speech, do you agree with them, or not?

Writing

1 Bassanio writes to his parents to ask their blessing on his marriage. He tells them of his feelings before, during and after the moment of choice. He tries to give some idea of what he thinks Portia felt at the time. He has to end with the sad news about Antonio and what he plans to do about it. Write the letter.
2 Jessica's thoughts and emotions are in turmoil. She has just 'gone over' to the other side. She has to cope with:
   - new religious ideas
   - new freedoms
   - a husband
   - a complete change of scene
   - her guilt in leaving her father (and stealing from him)
   - the weight of knowledge about her father's attitude and his influence on Antonio's fate.
   She arranges to meet her best friend and pours out her feelings. Write the conversation.

Quiz

1 Who quickly turns a day or two into a month or two?
2 If '*one half of me is yours, the other half yours*', whose am I?
3 Who plays the spider?
4 What colour eyes does jealousy have?
5 What colour are cowards' livers?
6 Try to fill in the gaps without looking up the speech. The first
   letters of the missing words, when unscrambled, make the
   name of one of the characters in the play.
   '.... *then, I am locked .. one of them,*
   If you do love me, you will find me out.
   .... and the ...., stand all aloof.
   Let music ..... while he doth make his choice;
   Then if he lose he makes a ....-like ...,
   Fading in music.'

**In a confrontation between Antonio and Shylock,
Antonio soon gives up hope of pleading with him.**

look to: keep a watch on him
gratis: without charging interest
naughty: worthless, useless
fond: foolish
abroad: out and about
dull-eyed fool: a fool easily-deceived
Christian intercessors: In the New Testament Christ is said to intercede, to plead with, his father for the salvation of sinful humans.
impenetrable: assuming that it is impossible to get through to him
bootless prayers: hopeless pleas
I oft...to me: I have often paid the bond due to him when his debtors appealed to me.

Scene 3

Venice

Enter SHYLOCK, SOLANIO, ANTONIO, *and Gaoler*

SHYLOCK	Gaoler, look to him, tell not me of mercy,
	This is the fool that lent out money gratis.
	Gaoler, look to him.
ANTONIO	Hear me yet good Shylock.
SHYLOCK	I'll have my bond, speak not against my bond,
	I have sworn an oath that I will have my bond.
	Thou call'dst me a dog before thou hadst a cause,
	But since I am a dog beware my fangs.
	The duke shall grant me justice. I do wonder,
	Thou naughty gaoler, that thou art so fond
	To come abroad with him at his request. 10
ANTONIO	I pray thee hear me speak.
SHYLOCK	I'll have my bond. I will not hear thee speak.
	I'll have my bond, and therefore speak no more.
	I'll not be made a soft and dull-eyed fool,
	To shake the head, relent, and sigh, and yield
	To Christian intercessors. Follow not;
	I'll have no speaking. I will have my bond. [*Exit*
SOLANIO	It is the most impenetrable cur
	That ever kept with men.
ANTONIO	Let him alone,
	I'll follow him no more with bootless prayers. 20
	He seeks my life, his reason well I know;
	I oft delivered from his forfeitures
	Many that have at times made moan to me;
	Therefore he hates me.
SOLANIO	I am sure the duke
	Will never grant this forfeiture to hold.
ANTONIO	The duke cannot deny the course of law.

The forfeit is due the following day. Antonio hopes
Bassanio will come.

---

commodity: commercial privileges. Antonio understands that
Venice, a city state whose wealth depends on trade with
many nations, cannot afford to make exceptions to its law,
or the whole basis of trust will be undermined.
bated: weakened

At Belmont, Lorenzo and Portia speak of Antonio and
Bassanio.

---

conceit: conception, understanding
god-like amity: divine friendship
Than...you: than normal kindness could make you feel
waste: spend
egal yoke: equal share
like: similar
lineaments: distinctive characteristics
bosom lover: close friend and confidant
needs: of necessity
How little...cruelty: How little is the amount I shall have
spent in buying the likeness of my soul out of the state to
which Shylock's devilish cruelty has condemned him.

For the commodity that strangers have
With us in Venice, if it be denied,
Will much impeach the justice of the state,
Since that the trade and profit of the city   30
Consisteth of all nations. Therefore go,
These griefs and losses have so bated me
That I shall hardly spare a pound of flesh
To-morrow, to my bloody creditor.
Well gaoler, on. Pray God Bassanio come
To see me pay his debt, and then I care not.

                                        [*Exeunt*

Scene 4

Belmont

Enter PORTIA, NERISSA, LORENZO, JESSICA, *and*
BALTHAZAR

LORENZO   Madam, although I speak it in your presence,
You have a noble and a true conceit
Of god-like amity, which appears most strongly
In bearing thus the absence of your lord.
But if you knew to whom you show this honour,
How true a gentleman you send relief,
How dear a lover of my lord your husband,
I know you would be prouder of the work
Than customary bounty can enforce you.

PORTIA   I never did repent for doing good,   10
Nor shall not now. For in companions
That do converse and waste the time together,
Whose souls do bear an egal yoke of love,
There must be needs a like proportion
Of lineaments, of manners, and of spirit;
Which makes me think that this Antonio,
Being the bosom lover of my lord,
Must needs be like my lord. If it be so,
How little is the cost I have bestowed

Portia tells Lorenzo that she and Nerissa have promised to remain in prayer and contemplation until their husbands return. The house is in his care. She sends her servant on an errand to Padua.

husbandry and manage: care and management
deny this imposition: refuse this task

1 Lorenzo agrees to look after the house, with Jessica. After exchanging farewells they leave.

1 ▷

2 Portia now sends her servant, Balthazar, to her cousin, Doctor Bellario in Padua, with instructions to bring her whatever notes and garments Bellario may give him.

2 ▷

In purchasing the semblance of my soul   20
From out the state of hellish cruelty.
This comes too near the praising of myself,
Therefore no more of it; hear other things.
Lorenzo I commit into your hands
The husbandry and manage of my house,
Until my lord's return. For mine own part
I have toward heaven breathed a secret vow
To live in prayer and contemplation,
Only attended by Nerissa here,
Until her husband and my lord's return.   30
There is a monastery two miles off,
And there will we abide. I do desire you
Not to deny this imposition,
The which my love and some necessity
Now lays upon you.

LORENZO   Madam, with all my heart,
I shall obey you in all fair commands.

PORTIA   My people do already know my mind,
And will acknowledge you and Jessica
In place of Lord Bassanio and myself.
So fare you well till we shall meet again.   40

LORENZO   Fair thoughts and happy hours attend on you.

JESSICA   I wish your ladyship all heart's content.

PORTIA   I thank you for your wish, and am well pleased
To wish it back on you. Fare you well Jessica.
                              [*Exeunt Jessica and Lorenzo*
Now Balthazar,
As I have ever found thee honest-true,
So let me find thee still. Take this same letter,
And use thou all the endeavour of a man
In speed to Padua. See thou render this
Into my cousin's hand, Doctor Bellario,   50
And look what notes and garments he doth give
    thee,
Bring them I pray thee with imagined speed

Portia tells Nerissa that they are to dress as young men and promises to tell her the rest of the plan on the way.

3 Portia assures Nerissa that they will shortly see their husbands again, but will not be recognized.

3 ▷

4 Portia is sure she will be the finer young gentleman of the two. She will get the voice right and will tell boastful lies of adventures with women.

4 ▷

5 They have to cover twenty miles that day and must be off, in Portia's coach.

5 ▷

	Unto the traject, to the common ferry
	Which trades to Venice. Waste no time in words
	But get thee gone. I shall be there before thee.
BALTHAZAR	Madam, I go with all convenient speed. [*Exit*
PORTIA	Come on Nerissa, I have work in hand
	That you yet know not of; we'll see our husbands
	Before they think of us.
NERISSA	Shall they see us?
PORTIA	They shall Nerissa; but in such a habit 60
	That they shall think we are accomplished
	With that we lack. I'll hold thee any wager,
	When we are both accoutred like young men,
	I'll prove the prettier fellow of the two,
	And wear my dagger with the braver grace,
	And speak between the change of man and boy
	With a reed voice, and turn two mincing steps
	Into a manly stride, and speak of frays
	Like a fine bragging youth; and tell quaint lies
	How honourable ladies sought my love, 70
	Which I denying, they fell sick and died–
	I could not do withal. Then I'll repent,
	And wish for all that, that I had not killed them;
	And twenty of these puny lies I'll tell,
	That men shall swear I have discontinued school
	Above a twelvemonth. I have within my mind
	A thousand raw tricks of these bragging Jacks,
	Which I will practise.
NERISSA	Why, shall we turn to men?
PORTIA	Fie, what a question's that, 80
	If thou wert near a lewd interpreter.
	But come, I'll tell thee all my whole device
	When I am in my coach, which stays for us
	At the park gate; and therefore haste away,
	For we must measure twenty miles today.
	[*Exeunt*

At Belmont, Launcelot is jokily assuring Jessica that she has no hope of going to heaven. Lorenzo joins them.

1 Because her father is a Jew, Launcelot asserts, Jessica will be damned. 1 ⟩

2 The only hope would be if she were not her father's daughter. Jessica points out that in this case her mother would have sinned. 2 ⟩

3 Launcelot now declares her damned on account of both her parents. (Scylla was a dangerous rock, home to a monster, and Charybdis a fierce whirlpool. They were situated opposite one another in the Straits of Messina and sailors had to steer between them.) 3 ⟩

4 Jessica claims she will be saved, because in marrying Lorenzo she became a Christian. 4 ⟩

5 Launcelot suggests that there were enough Christians before and any more will force the price of pork to go up – there will be more demand for it. 5 ⟩

6 Lorenzo, pretending jealousy, interrupts the nonsense. 6 ⟩

Scene 5

Belmont

Enter LAUNCELOT *and* JESSICA

LAUNCELOT   Yes truly; for look you, the sins of the father are to be laid upon the children, therefore I promise ye, I fear you. I was always plain with you, and so now I speak my agitation of the matter. Therefore be of good cheer, for truly I think you are damned. There is but one hope in it that can do you any good, and that is but a kind of bastard hope neither.

JESSICA   And what hope is that I pray thee?

LAUNCELOT   Marry you may partly hope that your father got you not, that you are not the Jew's daughter.   10

JESSICA   That were a kind of bastard hope indeed, so the sins of my mother should be visited upon me.

LAUNCELOT   Truly then I fear you are damned both by father and mother. Thus when I shun Scylla your father, I fall into Charybdis your mother; well, you are gone both ways.

JESSICA   I shall be saved by my husband, he hath made me a Christian.

LAUNCELOT   Truly the more to blame he, we were Christians enow before, e'en as many as could well live one   20 by another. This making of Christians will raise the price of hogs: if we grow all to be pork-eaters, we shall not shortly have a rasher on the coals for money.

Enter LORENZO

JESSICA   I'll tell my husband, Launcelot, what you say. Here he comes.

LORENZO   I shall grow jealous of you shortly Launcelot, if you

Lorenzo tells Launcelot to order dinner. This produces more witty nonsense from him. Lorenzo and Jessica are at last alone.

7 Jessica tells Lorenzo what they've been saying.

8 Lorenzo tries pleasantly to squash the irrepressible Launcelot by ordering dinner.

9 Lorenzo shows he has quite a soft spot for Launcelot.

10 He then asks Jessica whether she likes Portia.

thus get my wife into corners.

JESSICA   Nay, you need not fear us Lorenzo. Launcelot and I
           are out. He tells me flatly there is no mercy for   30
           me in heaven, because I am a Jew's daughter. And
           he says you are no good member of the
           commonwealth, for in converting Jews to
           Christians, you raise the price of pork.

LORENZO   I think the best grace of wit will shortly turn into
           silence, and discourse grow commendable in none
           only but parrots. Go in sirrah, bid them prepare for
           dinner.

LAUNCELOT That is done sir, they have all stomachs.

LORENZO   Goodly Lord, what a wit-snapper are you. Then   40
           bid them prepare dinner.

LAUNCELOT That is done too sir, only 'cover' is the word.

LORENZO   Will you cover then sir?

LAUNCELOT Not so sir neither, I know my duty.

LORENZO   Yet more quarrelling with occasion. Wilt thou show
           the whole wealth of thy wit in an instant? I pray
           thee understand a plain man in his plain meaning.
           Go to thy fellows, bid them cover the table, serve in
           the meat, and we will come in to dinner.

LAUNCELOT For the table sir, it shall be served in, for the   50
           meat sir, it shall be covered, for your coming in to
           dinner sir, why let it be as humours and conceits
           shall govern.   [*Exit*

LORENZO   O dear discretion, how his words are suited.
           The fool hath planted in his memory
           An army of good words, and I do know
           A many fools that stand in better place,
           Garnished like him, that for a tricksy word
           Defy the matter. How cheer'st thou Jessica?
           And now good sweet, say thy opinion,   60
           How dost thou like the Lord Bassanio's wife?

Jessica is very impressed with Portia. Lorenzo playfully tries to turn some of this praise on to himself.

11

11 Jessica thinks Bassanio is really fortunate in marrying Portia. He has the joys of heaven on earth. There is not another woman like her.

12 Lorenzo claims he is just such a husband. They go in to dinner.

12

 CTIVITIES

Keeping track

Scene 3

1 Antonio is now convinced that he knows the reason for Shylock's insistence on claiming his bond. What is this?
2 Why can the Duke not '*deny the course of law*' according to Antonio?
3 What change does Antonio see in himself?

JESSICA	Past all expressing. It is very meet
	The Lord Bassanio live an upright life,
	For having such a blessing in his lady,
	He finds the joys of heaven here on earth,
	And if on earth he do not merit it,
	In reason he should never come to heaven.
	Why, if two gods should play some heavenly
	match,
	And on the wager lay two earthly women,
	And Portia one, there must be something else 70
	Pawned with the other, for the poor rude world
	Hath not her fellow.
LORENZO	Even such a husband
	Hast thou of me, as she is for a wife.
JESSICA	Nay, but ask my opinion too of that.
LORENZO	I will anon, first let us go to dinner.
JESSICA	Nay, let me praise you while I have a stomach.
LORENZO	No pray thee, let it serve for table-talk,
	Then howsoe'er thou speak'st, 'mong other things
	I shall digest it.
JESSICA	Well, I'll set you forth. [*Exeunt*

Scene 4

4 What is Lorenzo's opinion of Antonio?
5 What does Portia tell Lorenzo she intends to do?
6 What does she ask Lorenzo and Jessica to do for her?
7 Why does Portia think Antonio and Bassanio must be alike?
8 Why do you think Portia and Nerissa intend to travel dressed as men?

Scene 5

9 In his jokey conversation with Jessica, why is Launcelot against the conversion of Jews to Christianity?

10 Does Jessica like Portia?

Discussion

1 Shylock refuses to consider the idea of **mercy,** but demands **justice.** Use a dictionary, a thesaurus, and your own ideas to decide what these words mean.
   - Is **mercy** the same as **forgiveness?**
   - Do you think it is easier to show **mercy** or to look for **revenge?**
   - Is **justice** the same as **fairness?**
   - Is true **justice** ever possible?
   - If you had done something wrong, would you prefer **justice** or **mercy?**

2 Why won't Shylock listen to Antonio in scene 3?

3 How do you think it possible that Antonio could come to be in prison for not repaying a loan? He was well-known and apparently well-loved. He had himself paid off people's debts. Why didn't his friends club together to rescue him? Why is it left to someone who didn't even know him to put up the money?

4 In scene 4 lines 60–78, Portia describes the disguise that she and Nerissa are to adopt. What is the picture that she paints of young men?

5 Does it seem likely that Portia is going to follow the expected behaviour for a wife?

Drama

1 In their club on the Rialto, the merchants, Antonio's friends, business acquaintances and rivals discuss the position he is in. There may be retired sea-captains there who have served in his ships, and one or two whose debts to Shylock he has paid off in the past.

   In groups of four or five, choose your character and your

attitude to Antonio's predicament. Do you think...
- it was rotten bad luck
- it's his own stupid fault, serve him right
- it's about time the rich man learnt what life is really like
- it'll be all right, the Duke will rescue him
- he's one of us, this grotesque forfeit can't happen
- he was always too soft on Bassanio?

Improvise the argument. Script the bits which sound good and play the result to the rest of the class. If a tape recorder is available, you could present it as part of a radio version of the play. Remember that in a heated discussion people hardly ever wait for someone to finish what they're saying!

2 We are not told exactly what disguise Portia and Nerissa use to travel to Venice. They have both seen several young men recently – the suitors – and they decide to model themselves on two of these.
- Read again what Portia says of her six suitors in Act 1.
- In groups of six, take one of the suitors each.
- Work on the pose each of these young men might take up.
- Make a group photograph (see page 209) of the six men so that Portia and Nerissa can choose which two they should copy.

Character

Scene 3

1 How does Antonio's attitude to his fate change in the course of this scene? Does this seem to you to be in character with your notes in his CHARACTER LOG so far? Has his feeling for Bassanio changed at all?

Scene 4

2 • Has Portia performed good deeds before?
- What does she have to say about friendship?
- What does she feel about Antonio, whom she has never met?
- Why does she feel like this?
- Is she sorry for Antonio?

- Antonio is Bassanio's best friend. What emotion might Portia feel now that she is married to Bassanio?
- What do you think she is going to be like as a wife?

3 Why do you think the people around him seem to like Launcelot? Some of the things he says to Jessica in scene 5 sound quite offensive. Why doesn't she take offence?

Close study

Scene 3 has three important points to make in preparation for the trial scene:

1 Shylock's present mood is established. So far we have only had it reported (Act 3 scene 2, lines 272–290). How does Shakespeare convey his mood?
- Look at the words Shylock uses to describe Antonio, the gaoler, and people who show mercy.
- Does he use devices such as repetition, or lists, which we have heard before? Make a note of any significant words or phrases.
- How does Shylock turn Antonio's previous choice of insult against him?

2 Antonio now speaks differently to Shylock. Both the words and the tone are different. Only two short sentences are needed to show this change. Make a note of them.

3 Antonio suddenly seems to resign himself to his fate. What two important realizations is this based on? Look at lines 8, 21–24, 26–31.

Writing

1 It would seem that Antonio is doomed. Imagine that you are an enthusiastic Venetian stone-mason who doesn't want to miss the opportunity of getting some work. Write an epitaph for Antonio.

2 Write the letter which Portia sends to her cousin, the lawyer Dr Bellario.

Quiz

Who:

1 *'never did repent for doing good'*?
2 will *'hardly spare a pound of flesh'*?
3 will have his bond?
4 will *'prove the prettier fellow of the two'*?
5 will *'grow jealous of Launcelot'*?

How many:

6 miles away is the monastery?
7 lies will Portia tell?
8 miles must they travel?

What:

9 will be in short supply?
10 must Balthazar bring?

The Duke arrives to preside over the decision to be made about the payment of Antonio's bond. He expresses sympathy with Antonio and assumes that Shylock will relent at last.

---

dram: drop
qualify: moderate
Out of...reach: out of reach of his malice
fashion: pretence
last hour of act: the eleventh hour
remorse: compassion
strange: remarkable

Act four

Scene 1 ————————

Venice

Enter the DUKE, *the Magnificoes,* ANTONIO,
BASSANIO, GRATIANO, SOLANIO, *and others*

DUKE	What, is Antonio here?
ANTONIO	Ready, so please your grace.
DUKE	I am sorry for thee, thou art come to answer
	A stony adversary, an inhuman wretch,
	Uncapable of pity, void and empty
	From any dram of mercy.

ANTONIO   I have heard
Your grace hath ta'en great pains to qualify
His rigorous course; but since he stands obdurate,
And that no lawful means can carry me
Out of his envy's reach, I do oppose   10
My patience to his fury, and am armed
To suffer with a quietness of spirit,
The very tyranny and rage of his.

DUKE	Go one and call the Jew into the court.
SOLANIO	He is ready at the door, he comes my lord.

Enter SHYLOCK

DUKE   Make room, and let him stand before our face.
Shylock, the world thinks, and I think so too,
That thou but leadest this fashion of thy malice
To the last hour of act, and then 'tis thought
Thou'lt show thy mercy and remorse more
          strange   20
Than is thy strange apparent cruelty;
And where thou now exacts the penalty,

The Duke tells Shylock that they are expecting him to be generous. Shylock replies that he has said what he intends to do, he has sworn it, and he will do it, purely because it suits him to do so – he hates Antonio.

loose the forfeiture: give up claim to the forfeit (the pound of flesh)

a moiety of the principal: a portion of the original sum loaned

enow: enough

And pluck...Tartars: The Duke suggests that Antonio's heavy losses have been so overwhelming that they should extract pity from the most hard-hearted.

Turks, and Tartars: notorious for cruel and barbaric behaviour

offices of tender courtesy: acts of civilized behaviour

possessed: informed

purpose: intend to do

humour: whim, fancy

baned: poisoned

gaping pig: boar's head. A dish served at table. The mouth would be open with an apple inside it.

affection: emotion

passion: strong feeling

rendered: given

but...shame: the man who passes water in public cannot help himself, although he is ashamed

lodged hate: settled, abiding hatred

Which is a pound of this poor merchant's flesh,
Thou wilt not only loose the forfeiture,
But touched with human gentleness and love,
Forgive a moiety of the principal,
Glancing an eye of pity on his losses
That have of late so huddled on his back,
Enow to press a royal merchant down,
And pluck commiseration of his state   30
From brassy bosoms and rough hearts of flint,
From stubborn Turks, and Tartars never trained
To offices of tender courtesy.
We all expect a gentle answer Jew.

SHYLOCK   I have possessed your grace of what I purpose;
And by our holy Sabbath have I sworn
To have the due and forfeit of my bond.
If you deny it, let the danger light
Upon your charter and your city's freedom.
You'll ask me why I rather choose to have   40
A weight of carrion flesh, than to receive
Three thousand ducats. I'll not answer that,
But say it is my humour; is it answered?
What if my house be troubled with a rat,
And I be pleased to give ten thousand ducats
To have it baned? What, are you answered yet?
Some men there are love not a gaping pig;
Some that are mad if they behold a cat;
And others when the bagpipe sings i' the nose,
Cannot contain their urine; for affection,   50
Mistress of passion, sways it to the mood
Of what it likes or loathes. Now for your answer:
As there is no firm reason to be rendered
Why he cannot abide a gaping pig;
Why he, a harmless necessary cat;
Why he, a woollen bagpipe; but of force
Must yield to such inevitable shame,
As to offend, himself being offended;
So can I give no reason, nor I will not,
More than a lodged hate and a certain loathing   60

Bassanio argues with Shylock. Antonio knows there is no point in this. Bassanio offers twice the loan. Shylock refuses. He insists on having what he has 'bought'.

---

losing suit: winning the case will lose him the money
think: bear in mind
main flood: high tide
bate: reduce
fretten: buffeted
with...conveniency: with simple proceedings and all decent speed
draw: accept
in abject...parts: in miserable and servile tasks

I bear Antonio, that I follow thus
A losing suit against him. Are you answered?

BASSANIO This is no answer thou unfeeling man,
To excuse the current of thy cruelty.

SHYLOCK I am not bound to please thee with my answer.

BASSANIO Do all men kill the things they do not love?

SHYLOCK Hates any man the thing he would not kill?

BASSANIO Every offence is not a hate at first.

SHYLOCK What, wouldst thou have a serpent sting thee twice?

ANTONIO I pray you think you question with the Jew.   70
You may as well go stand upon the beach
And bid the main flood bate his usual height;
You may as well use question with the wolf
Why he hath made the ewe bleat for the lamb;
You may as well forbid the mountain pines
To wag their high tops and to make no noise
When they are fretten with the gusts of heaven;
You may as well do any thing most hard
As seek to soften that—than which what's harder?—
His Jewish heart. Therefore I do beseech you   80
Make no moe offers, use no farther means,
But with all brief and plain conveniency
Let me have judgement, and the Jew his will.

BASSANIO For thy three thousand ducats here is six.

SHYLOCK If every ducat in six thousand ducats
Were in six parts, and every part a ducat,
I would not draw them, I would have my bond.

DUKE How shalt thou hope for mercy, rendering none?

SHYLOCK What judgement shall I dread, doing no wrong?
You have among you many a purchased slave,   90
Which like your asses, and your dogs and mules,
You use in abject and in slavish parts,
Because you bought them, shall I say to you,
Let them be free, marry them to your heirs?

Shylock suggests that the law of Venice will be worthless if he cannot have judgement. Bassanio sees hope in the arrival of a messenger from Padua. Nerissa presents a letter while Shylock sharpens his knife on the sole of his shoe.

burthens: burdens, heavy loads
viands: food
stays without: is waiting outside
new come: just arrived
tainted wether: sick ram (*wether* often means a castrated ram)
Meetest for death: best killed
live still: go on living
whet: sharpen

	Why sweat they under burthens? Let their beds
	Be made as soft as yours, and let their palates
	Be seasoned with such viands. You will answer,
	'The slaves are ours'; so do I answer you.
	The pound of flesh which I demand of him
	Is dearly bought, 'tis mine and I will have it.

Why sweat they under burthens? Let their beds
Be made as soft as yours, and let their palates
Be seasoned with such viands. You will answer,
'The slaves are ours'; so do I answer you.
The pound of flesh which I demand of him
Is dearly bought, 'tis mine and I will have it.   100
If you deny me, fie upon your law,
There is no force in the decrees of Venice.
I stand for judgement–answer, shall I have it?

DUKE   Upon my power I may dismiss this court,
Unless Bellario a learned doctor,
Whom I have sent for to determine this,
Come here today.

SOLANIO   My lord, here stays without
A messenger with letters from the doctor,
New come from Padua.

DUKE   Bring us the letters. Call the messenger.   110

BASSANIO Good cheer Antonio. What man, courage yet.
The Jew shall have my flesh, blood, bones, and all,
Ere thou shalt lose for me one drop of blood.

ANTONIO   I am a tainted wether of the flock,
Meetest for death. The weakest kind of fruit
Drops earliest to the ground, and so let me.
You cannot better be employed Bassanio,
Than to live still and write mine epitaph.

Enter NERISSA, *dressed like a lawyer's clerk*

DUKE   Came you from Padua, from Bellario?

NERISSA   From both, my lord. Bellario greets your grace.   120
                              [*Presents a letter*

BASSANIO Why dost thou whet thy knife so earnestly?

SHYLOCK   To cut the forfeiture from that bankrupt there.

GRATIANO Not on thy sole, but on thy soul, harsh Jew,
Thou mak'st thy knife keen. But no metal can,
No, not the hangman's axe, bear half the keenness

Gratiano now tries insults but Shylock insists he will have his legal rights. The letter from Bellario introduces Balthazar, otherwise known as Portia.

envy: malice
pierce: get through to
wit: intelligence
inexecrable: most accursed
for...accused: justice is at fault, seeing that you are still alive
my faith: the faith of a Christian
hold opinion: agree
Pythagoras: the Greek philosopher and mathematician (sixth century BC). He believed in the transmigration of souls – the idea that in a process of purification (or punishment) a person's soul on their death can enter the body of another person or an animal, and an animal's soul can enter another animal or a person.
infuse: pour, instil
trunks: bodies
fell: deadly
fleet: pass away (from his body)
whilst...dam: while you still lay inside your pagan mother's womb
Till thou...bond: until you can get the seal off my bond by complaining so bitterly
Thou but offendest: you're only damaging
wit: intellect
cureless: incurable

1 Bellario's letter has recommended a young and learned doctor of law to the Duke.
2 Portia is waiting outside until called.
3 In his letter Bellario claims he is ill but that as the '*young doctor of Rome*' was paying him a friendly visit when the Duke's messenger arrived to seek his opinion, they both looked for similar cases in his law books.
4 The young visitor is now bringing the results of these researches, together with his own and Bellario's opinions on the case.

	Of thy sharp envy. Can no prayers pierce thee?
SHYLOCK	No, none that thou hast wit enough to make.

GRATIANO   O, be thou damned, inexecrable dog,
And for thy life let justice be accused.
Thou almost mak'st me waver in my faith,   130
To hold opinion with Pythagoras,
That souls of animals infuse themselves
Into the trunks of men. Thy currish spirit
Governed a wolf, who hanged for human slaughter,
Even from the gallows did his fell soul fleet,
And whilst thou layest in thy unhallowed dam,
Infused itself in thee; for thy desires
Are wolvish, bloody, starved, and ravenous.

SHYLOCK   Till thou canst rail the seal from off my bond,
Thou but offendest thy lungs to speak so loud.   140
Repair thy wit good youth, or it will fall
To cureless ruin. I stand here for law.

DUKE   This letter from Bellario doth commend
A young and learned doctor to our court.
Where is he?

NERISSA   He attendeth here hard by
To know your answer whether you'll admit him.

DUKE   With all my heart. Some three or four of you
Go give him courteous conduct to this place.
Meantime the court shall hear Bellario's letter.

CLERK   [*Reads*] 'Your grace shall understand that at the   150
receipt of your letter I am very sick, but in the
instant that your messenger came, in loving
visitation was with me a young doctor of Rome; his
name is Balthazar. I acquainted him with the cause
in controversy between the Jew and Antonio the
merchant; we turned o'er many books together; he
is furnished with my opinion, which bettered with
his own learning, the greatness whereof I cannot
enough commend, comes with him at my
importunity, to fill up your grace's request in   160

Once the letter has been read, Portia is admitted to the
court and meets the protagonists. She too suggests
Shylock should show mercy, and gives her definition of
the word.

5 Bellario says the Duke should not mistrust the lawyer's
youth.
6 The Duke asks Portia whether she has studied the current
dispute in his court.
7 Portia acquaints herself with Shylock and Antonio,
indicating already that Shylock has a valid case.

5

Then must...merciful: the Jew has to show mercy
quality: nature
is not strained: cannot be forced
becomes: suits

6

7

     my stead. I beseech you let his lack of years be no
     impediment to let him lack a reverend estimation,
     for I never knew so young a body with so old a
     head. I leave him to your gracious acceptance,
     whose trial shall better publish his commendation.'

DUKE You hear the learned Bellario what he writes,
     And here, I take it, is the doctor come.

Enter PORTIA, *dressed like a doctor of laws*

     Give me your hand. Come you from old Bellario?

PORTIA I did my lord.

DUKE   You are welcome, take your place.
     Are you acquainted with the difference   170
     That holds this present question in the court?

PORTIA I am informed throughly of the cause.
     Which is the merchant here? And which the Jew?

DUKE Antonio and old Shylock, both stand forth.

PORTIA Is your name Shylock?

SHYLOCK   Shylock is my name.

PORTIA Of a strange nature is the suit you follow,
     Yet in such rule that the Venetian law
     Cannot impugn you as you do proceed.
     You stand within his danger, do you not?

ANTONIO Ay, so he says.

PORTIA   Do you confess the bond? 180

ANTONIO I do.

PORTIA   Then must the Jew be merciful.

SHYLOCK On what compulsion must I? Tell me that.

PORTIA The quality of mercy is not strained,
     It droppeth as the gentle rain from heaven
     Upon the place beneath. It is twice blest,
     It blesseth him that gives, and him that takes.
     'Tis mightiest in the mightiest, it becomes
     The throned monarch better than his crown.

Portia continues with her definition of mercy. Shylock still demands 'justice' and refuses Bassanio's offers of money and self-sacrifice. As Portia upholds the law, Shylock is jubilant.

temporal: earthly, secular (as opposed to religious)
attribute to: symbol of
sceptred sway: temporal rule
attribute to: quality, characteristic of
seasons: moderates
And...prayer: the Lord's Prayer
My deeds...head: Shylock takes full responsibility for his actions
discharge: pay
tender: offer
malice...truth: evil intent overwhelms righteousness
once: just this once. Bassanio is suggesting that on this occasion the doctor could use his authority to give the law a slightly more liberal interpretation.
curb: check, frustrate
of his will: from getting what he wants
precedent: an example of a judgement on which later cases may then be based
Daniel: a reference to the story of Susannah in the Apocrypha. She was accused of immoral behaviour by two elders, whose advances she had rejected. He questioned them separately and was able to prove they were lying. They were put to death.

His sceptre shows the force of temporal power,
The attribute to awe and majesty,   190
Wherein doth sit the dread and fear of kings.
But mercy is above this sceptred sway,
It is enthroned in the hearts of kings,
It is an attribute to God himself;
And earthly power doth then show likest God's
When mercy seasons justice. Therefore Jew,
Though justice be thy plea, consider this,
That in the course of justice, none of us
Should see salvation. We do pray for mercy,
And that same prayer doth teach us all to render 200
The deeds of mercy. I have spoke thus much
To mitigate the justice of thy plea,
Which if thou follow, this strict court of Venice
Must needs give sentence 'gainst the merchant there.

SHYLOCK   My deeds upon my head, I crave the law,
            The penalty and forfeit of my bond.

PORTIA   Is he not able to discharge the money?

BASSANIO   Yes, here I tender it for him in the court,
            Yea, twice the sum, if that will not suffice,
            I will be bound to pay it ten times o'er   210
            On forfeit of my hands, my head, my heart.
            If this will not suffice, it must appear
            That malice bears down truth. And I beseech
                you
            Wrest once the law to your authority:
            To do a great right, do a little wrong,
            And curb this cruel devil of his will.

PORTIA   It must not be, there is no power in Venice
            Can alter a decree establishèd.
            'Twill be recorded for a precedent,
            And many an error by the same example   220
            Will rush into the state. It cannot be.

SHYLOCK   A Daniel come to judgement. Yea a Daniel.
            O wise young judge, how I do honour thee.

PORTIA   I pray you let me look upon the bond.

Although Portia mentions three times the sum and asks for mercy, Shylock cannot be moved. The bond must stand and Antonio must get ready to lose a pound of flesh.

---

perjury: usually refers to the telling of a lie when a person has sworn to tell the truth. Here the suggestion is that Shylock will not go back on the oath he apparently took in the synagogue, witnessed by Tubal, to take vengeance on Antonio (Act 3 scene 1, line 124).

tenour: the actual wording of a legal document

exposition: explanation, setting out of the facts

Whereof you are...pillar: of which you deserve to be seen as a strong supporter. (A 'pillar of society' is a well-known member of society, who upholds its values.)

stay: make my stand

intent: meaning

SHYLOCK	Here 'tis, most reverend doctor, here it is.
PORTIA	Shylock there's thrice thy money offered thee.
SHYLOCK	An oath, an oath, I have an oath in heaven.
	Shall I lay perjury upon my soul?
	No, not for Venice.
PORTIA	Why this bond is forfeit,
	And lawfully by this the Jew may claim 230
	A pound of flesh, to be by him cut off
	Nearest the merchant's heart. Be merciful,
	Take thrice thy money, bid me tear the bond.
SHYLOCK	When it is paid according to the tenour.
	It doth appear you are a worthy judge;
	You know the law, your exposition
	Hath been most sound. I charge you by the law,
	Whereof you are a well-deserving pillar,
	Proceed to judgement. By my soul I swear
	There is no power in the tongue of man 240
	To alter me, I stay here on my bond.
ANTONIO	Most heartily I do beseech the court
	To give the judgement.
PORTIA	Why then thus it is:
	You must prepare your bosom for his knife.
SHYLOCK	O noble judge, O excellent young man.
PORTIA	For the intent and purpose of the law
	Hath full relation to the penalty,
	Which here appeareth due upon the bond.
SHYLOCK	'Tis very true. O wise and upright judge,
	How much more elder art thou than thy looks. 250
PORTIA	Therefore lay bare your bosom.
SHYLOCK	Ay, his breast,
	So says the bond, doth it not noble judge?
	'Nearest his heart', those are the very words.
PORTIA	It is so. Are there balance here to weigh
	The flesh?

Portia expects there to be a surgeon, to prevent Antonio from bleeding to death. Antonio gives what he thinks is his last speech. Bassanio declares he would sacrifice his wife and everything else for Antonio's life. Gratiano joins in.

on your charge: at your expense
armed: resolved, settled in my mind
use: habit, practice
the process of Antonio's end: how Antonio met his end (with a play on words, since '*process*' can mean 'trial')
speak me fair: speak well of me
Repent/repents: regret/regrets
with all my heart: he means emotionally and literally, making a brave joke just before his death
esteemed: valued

SHYLOCK	I have them ready.
PORTIA	Have by some surgeon Shylock, on your charge,
	To stop his wounds, lest he do bleed to death.
SHYLOCK	Is it so nominated in the bond?
PORTIA	It is not so expressed, but what of that?
	'Twere good you do so much for charity. 260
SHYLOCK	I cannot find it, 'tis not in the bond.
PORTIA	You merchant, have you any thing to say?
ANTONIO	But little; I am armed and well prepared.
	Give me your hand Bassanio, fare you well.
	Grieve not that I am fallen to this for you;
	For herein Fortune shows herself more kind
	Than is her custom: it is still her use
	To let the wretched man outlive his wealth,
	To view with hollow eye and wrinkled brow
	An age of poverty; from which lingering
	penance 270
	Of such misery doth she cut me off.
	Commend me to your honourable wife.
	Tell her the process of Antonio's end.
	Say how I loved you, speak me fair in death;
	And when the tale is told, bid her be judge
	Whether Bassanio had not once a love.
	Repent but you that you shall lose your friend,
	And he repents not that he pays your debt.
	For if the Jew do cut but deep enough,
	I'll pay it presently with all my heart. 280
BASSANIO	Antonio, I am married to a wife
	Which is as dear to me as life itself,
	But life itself, my wife, and all the world,
	Are not with me esteemed above thy life.
	I would lose all, ay sacrifice them all
	Here to this devil, to deliver you.
PORTIA	Your wife would give you little thanks for that,
	If she were by to hear you make the offer.
GRATIANO	I have a wife whom I protest I love,

Portia declares the law says Shylock may take his pound of flesh – but no blood. Shylock tries to settle for the offer of nine thousand ducats.

Entreat: beg for
else: otherwise
Barrabas: the thief (a Jew) whom the crowd asked Pontius Pilate to release instead of Jesus
Tarry: wait
urgest: press for, demand

	I would she were in heaven, so she could 290

I would she were in heaven, so she could   290
Entreat some power to change this currish Jew.

NERISSA 'Tis well you offer it behind her back,
The wish would make else an unquiet house.

SHYLOCK [*Aside*] These be the Christian husbands. I have a
daughter–
Would any of the stock of Barrabas
Had been her husband rather than a Christian.
[*Aloud*] We trifle time, I pray thee pursue sentence.

PORTIA A pound of that same merchant's flesh is thine;
The court awards it, and the law doth give it.

SHYLOCK Most rightful judge.   300

PORTIA And you must cut this flesh from off his breast;
The law allows it, and the court awards it.

SHYLOCK Most learned judge. A sentence. Come prepare.

PORTIA Tarry a little, there is something else.
This bond doth give thee here no jot of blood,
The words expressly are 'a pound of flesh'.
Take then thy bond, take thou thy pound of flesh,
But in the cutting it, if thou dost shed
One drop of Christian blood, thy lands and
goods
Are by the laws of Venice confiscate   310
Unto the state of Venice.

GRATIANO O upright judge–mark, Jew–O learned judge.

SHYLOCK Is that the law?

PORTIA   Thyself shalt see the act.
For as thou urgest justice, be assured
Thou shalt have justice more than thou desirest.

GRATIANO O learned judge–mark, Jew–a learned judge.

SHYLOCK I take this offer then; pay the bond thrice
And let the Christian go.

BASSANIO   Here is the money.

Portia announces the penalty if Shylock takes more or less than his bond. Gratiano gloats. Shylock has now lost even the original loan. He wants to leave but there is now a case against him.

Soft: wait
all justice: everything the law provides for
soft, no haste: just a moment, there's no hurry
scruple: a minute amount
I have you...hip: Gratiano has Shylock at a disadvantage. (See note on Act 1 scene 3 line 43)
at thy peril: at your own risk
Tarry: wait
alien: non-Venetian
seek the life: tries to kill
contrive: plot

PORTIA	Soft.
	The Jew shall have all justice–soft, no haste– 320
	He shall have nothing but the penalty.
GRATIANO	O Jew, an upright judge, a learned judge.
PORTIA	Therefore prepare thee to cut off the flesh.
	Shed thou no blood, nor cut thou less nor more
	But just a pound of flesh. If thou tak'st more
	Or less than a just pound, be it but so much
	As makes it light or heavy in the substance,
	Of the division of the twentieth part
	Of one poor scruple, nay if the scale do turn
	But in the estimation of a hair, 330
	Thou diest, and all thy goods are confiscate.
GRATIANO	A second Daniel, a Daniel, Jew.
	Now, infidel, I have you on the hip.
PORTIA	Why doth the Jew pause? Take thy forfeiture.
SHYLOCK	Give me my principal, and let me go.
BASSANIO	I have it ready for thee, here it is.
PORTIA	He hath refused it in the open court.
	He shall have merely justice and his bond.
GRATIANO	A Daniel still say I, a second Daniel.
	I thank thee Jew for teaching me that word. 340
SHYLOCK	Shall I not have barely my principal?
PORTIA	Thou shalt have nothing but the forfeiture
	To be so taken at thy peril Jew.
SHYLOCK	Why then the devil give him good of it.
	I'll stay no longer question.
PORTIA	Tarry Jew,
	The law hath yet another hold on you.
	It is enacted in the laws of Venice,
	If it be proved against an alien
	That by direct, or indirect attempts
	He seek the life of any citizen, 350
	The party 'gainst the which he doth contrive
	Shall seize one half his goods, the other half

The tables have been turned on Shylock. He is in danger of death or ruin. Portia asks Antonio what mercy he can grant. He is concerned to help Lorenzo and Jessica.

privy coffer of the state: the treasury that belongs entirely and only to the state

manifest proceeding: quite obvious actions

formerly by me rehearsed: mentioned by me earlier

And yet thy...cord: because all your possessions now belong to the state you cannot even afford a length of rope

spirit: attitude

humbleness may...fine: a sufficiently humble attitude may allow us to reduce it to a fine

Ay...Antonio: the state's share can be reduced to a fine, but not Antonio's

house: '*house*' means both 'dwelling' and also 'family' with a memory of ancestors and a consciousness of descendants to come, all belonging to it

a halter gratis: a noose for free

to quit the fine: to do away with the fine

so: provided that

in use: in trust

Comes to the privy coffer of the state,
And the offender's life lies in the mercy
Of the duke only, 'gainst all other voice.
In which predicament I say thou stand'st;
For it appears by manifest proceeding,
That indirectly, and directly too,
Thou hast contrived against the very life
Of the defendant; and thou hast incurred   360
The danger formerly by me rehearsed.
Down therefore, and beg mercy of the duke.

GRATIANO   Beg that thou mayst have leave to hang thyself.
And yet thy wealth being forfeit to the state,
Thou has not left the value of a cord,
Therefore thou must be hanged at the state's
        charge.

DUKE   That thou shalt see the difference of our spirit,
I pardon thee thy life before thou ask it.
For half thy wealth, it is Antonio's,
The other half comes to the general state,   370
Which humbleness may drive unto a fine.

PORTIA   Ay, for the state, not for Antonio.

SHYLOCK   Nay, take my life and all, pardon not that.
You take my house, when you do take the prop
That doth sustain my house; you take my life,
When you do take the means whereby I live.

PORTIA   What mercy can you render him Antonio?

GRATIANO   A halter gratis, nothing else for God's sake.

ANTONIO   So please my lord the duke and all the court
To quit the fine for one half of his goods,   380
I am content—so he will let me have
The other half in use—to render it
Upon his death unto the gentleman
That lately stole his daughter.
Two things provided more, that for this favour,
He presently become a Christian;

Shylock is forced to provide for his daughter and Lorenzo. He claims he feels ill and is given leave to go. Portia refuses the Duke's invitation to dinner. She receives Bassanio's and Antonio's thanks.

---

record a gift: sign over as a gift

recant: take back

ten more: ten more would make up the twelve needed for a jury. In a rather sick joke, juries were sometimes called 'godfathers', because if they decided the defendant was guilty of a capital offence they were sending him 'to God'.

1 The Duke invites Balthazar/Portia to dine with him.   1 ▷

2 She says she has to leave at once for Padua.   2 ▷

3 The Duke tells Antonio to reward Balthazar as he is deeply indebted to him.   3 ▷

4 Bassanio thanks Balthazar.   4 ▷

5 Bassanio then offers the wise lawyer the three thousand ducats which were not repaid to Shylock.   5 ▷

6 Portia says she is well paid by the result.   6 ▷

	The other, that he do record a gift Here in the court of all he dies possessed Unto his son Lorenzo and his daughter.	
DUKE	He shall do this, or else I do recant The pardon that I late pronouncèd here.	390
PORTIA	Art thou contented Jew? What dost thou say?	
SHYLOCK	I am content.	
PORTIA	Clerk, draw a deed of gift.	
SHYLOCK	I pray you give me leave to go from hence, I am not well. Send the deed after me, And I will sign it.	
DUKE	Get thee gone, but do it.	
GRATIANO	In christening shalt thou have two godfathers; Had I been judge, thou shouldst have had ten more, To bring thee to the gallows, not to the font.	

[Exit Shylock

DUKE	Sir I entreat you home with me to dinner.	400
PORTIA	I humbly do desire your grace of pardon, I must away this night toward Padua, And it is meet I presently set forth.	
DUKE	I am sorry that your leisure serves you not. Antonio, gratify this gentleman, For in my mind you are much bound to him.	

[Exeunt Duke and his train

BASSANIO	Most worthy gentleman, I and my friend Have by your wisdom been this day acquitted Of grievous penalties, in lieu whereof Three thousand ducats due unto the Jew, We freely cope your courteous pains withal.	410
ANTONIO	And stand indebted over and above In love and service to you evermore.	
PORTIA	He is well paid that is well satisfied, And I, delivering you, am satisfied	

Antonio and Bassanio press the lawyer to accept a gift. Portia asks at last for Bassanio's ring. He refuses and 'offends' her.

7

7 She takes her leave, saying he must '*know*' her when they meet again (in all senses of the word).

of force...further: I really must try again to influence you
remembrance: memento
tribute: gift
to pardon me: to pardon me for insisting
trifle: trinket
There's more...value: more hangs on this (giving up the ring) than on its monetary value
proclamation: public announcement
'scuse: excuse

	And therein do account myself well paid.
	My mind was never yet more mercenary.
	I pray you, know me when we meet again.
	I wish you well, and so I take my leave.
BASSANIO	Dear sir, of force I must attempt you further: 420
	Take some remembrance of us as a tribute,
	Not as a fee. Grant me two things I pray you,
	Not to deny me, and to pardon me.
PORTIA	You press me far, and therefore I will yield.
	[*To Antonio*] Give me your gloves, I'll wear them for your sake.
	[*To Bassanio*] And for your love I'll take this ring from you.
	Do not draw back your hand, I'll take no more,
	And you in love shall not deny me this.
BASSANIO	This ring good sir, alas, it is a trifle,
	I will not shame myself to give you this. 430
PORTIA	I will have nothing else but only this,
	And now methinks I have a mind to it.
BASSANIO	There's more depends on this than on the value.
	The dearest ring in Venice will I give you,
	And find it out by proclamation.
	Only for this, I pray you, pardon me.
PORTIA	I see sir, you are liberal in offers.
	You taught me first to beg, and now methinks
	You teach me how a beggar should be answered.
BASSANIO	Good sir, this ring was given me by my wife, 440
	And when she put it on, she made me vow
	That I should neither sell, nor give, nor lose it.
PORTIA	That 'scuse serves many men to save their gifts.
	An if your wife be not a mad-woman,
	And know how well I have deserved the ring,
	She would not hold out enemy for ever
	For giving it to me. Well, peace be with you.

[*Exeunt Portia and Nerissa*

Bassanio sends Gratiano after Portia with the ring. They plan to hurry to Belmont.

1 >

2 >

1 Antonio persuades Bassanio to let the lawyer have the ring.
2 Gratiano is instructed to catch Portia up and give her the ring.

3 The following day they, with Antonio, will make all speed they can to Belmont.

3 >

Gratiano hands over Bassanio's ring – Nerissa plans to get hers from him.

1 Portia and Nerissa have had the deed of gift drawn up for Shylock to sign. Nerissa is to deliver it to him. They plan to set off for home immediately afterwards.

1 >

2 Portia accepts her ring from Gratiano.

2 >

3 While Gratiano guides Nerissa to Shylock's house she will try to persuade him to part with her ring.

3 >

ANTONIO   My Lord Bassanio, let him have the ring.
           Let his deservings and my love withal
           Be valued 'gainst your wife's commandment.   450

BASSANIO   Go Gratiano, run and overtake him,
           Give him the ring, and bring him if thou canst
           Unto Antonio's house; away, make haste.

                                    [*Exit Gratiano*

           Come, you and I will thither presently,
           And in the morning early will we both
           Fly toward Belmont. Come Antonio.

                                              [*Exeunt*

Scene ②

Venice

Enter PORTIA *and* NERISSA

PORTIA   Inquire the Jew's house out, give him this deed,
           And let him sign it; we'll away tonight,
           And be a day before our husbands home.
           This deed will be well welcome to Lorenzo.

           Enter GRATIANO

GRATIANO   Fair sir, you are well o'erta'en.
           My Lord Bassanio upon more advice,
           Hath sent you here this ring, and doth entreat
           Your company at dinner.

PORTIA   That cannot be.
           His ring I do accept most thankfully,
           And so I pray you tell him. Furthermore,   10
           I pray you show my youth old Shylock's house.

GRATIANO   That will I do.

NERISSA   Sir, I would speak with you.
           [*Aside to Portia*] I'll see if I can get my husband's
               ring
           Which I did make him swear to keep for ever.

Portia predicts they will get the better of their husbands. [4]

4 Portia is sure Nerissa will manage to get her ring too. [5]
5 Although their husbands will swear that they gave their rings to men, Portia and Nerissa will know better.

CTIVITIES

Keeping track

Scene 1

1 What does the Duke hope Shylock intends to do?
2 What does Shylock intend to do?
3 What reason does he give?
4 Why does Antonio seem eager for the final judgement?
5 What reason does Bellario give for an unknown lawyer's appearance in court?
6 Why must the law be allowed to stand?
7 What loophole does Portia find in the wording of the bond?
8 What penalties does Shylock have to pay?
9 How do Lorenzo and Jessica gain by the result?
10 What reward does Portia claim?

Scene 2

11 What invitation does Portia refuse?
12 What does Nerissa plan to get?

Discussion

1 The Duke is to act as judge. Is he unbiased and fair?
   • He speaks to Antonio before Shylock appears. What does he say about Shylock?
   • How does he speak to Shylock? Is he making judgements

PORTIA   [*Aside to Nerissa*] Thou mayst, I warrant. We shall
               have old swearing
               That they did give the rings away to men;
               But we'll outface them, and outswear them too.
               Away, make haste, thou know'st where I will tarry.

NERISSA   Come good sir, will you show me to this house?
                                                              [*Exeunt*

---

about Shylock's intentions?
   • Look back at earlier scenes for evidence of the Duke's
     attitude towards other people. (Act 3 scene 2 lines
     279–284).
   • Do we learn anything about the Duke's attitude after
     Portia's judgement?
2 Shylock says '*I stand for judgement*' (scene 1 line 103). Do you
   think that Shylock is trying to prove a point or does he simply
   want to see Antonio dead? List as many reasons as you can for
   Shylock's behaviour. Is there any justification for it?
3 Look at Portia's speech which begins '*The quality of mercy is not
   strained...*' How does she try to persuade Shylock to show
   mercy?
   • Read the speech carefully and look at what Portia actually
     says about mercy.
   • Make your own list of the points she makes.
   • Are her comments about God and salvation likely to move
     Shylock (scene 1 line 192 onwards)?
4 Portia has spoken very movingly about the quality of mercy.
   She shows later (scene 1 lines 345–362) that Shylock has
   committed an offence against Venetian law. How much mercy
   do you think is shown to Shylock?

Drama

Portrait of Shylock

1 After the trial is over, Gratiano commissions a painting entitled 'The Evil Shylock' to reflect his very extreme and intolerant feelings about Shylock expressed in Act 4 scene 1. The moment he wishes to capture is when Shylock takes out his knife and starts to sharpen it.

   • Working in a group of eight to ten, create the painting which you think will please Gratiano.
   • Think about all the characters who would be present and how they would be looking at Shylock.
   • Think about the shape of the composition. Which characters are standing, bending, kneeling, sitting? Is Shylock at the centre, or to one side?

2 Tubal, Shylock's friend, has heard about this painting. With a group of friends he also commissions a painting to give a more sympathetic view of what happened.

   • Which part of the scene might he wish to show?
   • What title would he wish to give this painting?
   • Work on this painting in the ways suggested above.

The quality of mercy

Read Portia's speech, scene 1 lines 183–204. Work in a group of five or six.

• One member of the group takes the role of Shylock.
• Divide up Portia's lines among the remaining members of the group.
• Practise your lines and learn them.
• Place Shylock in the middle of a circle.
• As the members of the group say their lines, they step towards Shylock.
• All the members of the group constantly look hard at Shylock.
• He looks steadfastly back at whoever is speaking.
• Before saying his lines he must make eye contact with every person, one at a time.

Experiment with pace and volume.

Follow up

As a whole-class activity.

- All the Shylocks should be in the centre.
- All group members who have learnt the same lines should re-group together.
- Repeat the activity on this larger scale.

Blood

Use FORUM THEATRE (page 210) to explore the exchange between Portia and Shylock when she traps him into saying there is no reference to blood in the agreement (Act 4 scene 1 lines 256–261).

- How can this be done so that the audience knows what Portia is doing, but Antonio and Shylock, at least, remain unaware of her cleverness?
- Does anyone realize what she is doing?
- Who might this be?
- How could it be shown?

Character

1 Shylock makes his last appearance in Act 4 scene 1, so your CHARACTER LOG on Shylock will end here.
   - How does he behave when he thinks he is winning?
   - Is his behaviour what you have come to expect of him so far? Look carefully at his one-line answers, as well as at his longer speeches. Look too at his reply to Gratiano (scene 1 lines 139–142).
   - Why do lines 40–46 in scene 1 offer a particularly chilling comparison? What is Shylock saying?
     Compare line 67, in scene 1.
   - How does Shylock react when he becomes the victim?
2 What qualities (good or bad) does Gratiano show in this scene?
3 Continue with your CHARACTER LOG of Portia.
   - What new qualities do we see in her in this scene?
   - Do you admire her, or find her cruel?

Close study

Scene 1 lines 70–80

1 Antonio does not just tell Bassanio that it is useless to plead with Shylock. He gives us three short pictures, images, of other attempts that would be useless.
   - What are they?
   - What do they tell us about one of Shakespeare's interests?
   - Do you think this is an effective way of demonstrating the problem?
   - The pictures give very extreme examples. Each one is absolutely impossible. What influence does this have on how you expect the rest of the scene to develop?
   - Something else the images do is to take us for a moment outside the courtroom – to the coast, the field, the hilltop. Is this a welcome breath of fresh air, or an unnecessary distraction?

Scene 1 lines 90–100

2 Shylock, too, uses vivid comparisons when he wants to make a point.
   - What example does he use to illustrate the fact that the pound of flesh is his: *''tis mine and I will have it'*?
   - It is a much longer comparison than any of the three Antonio has used. Which do you find more striking?

Writing

1 Imagine that you are the clerk of the court. You have to keep an accurate record of the main events of the trial to present to the Duke afterwards. Write this record. It should contain only facts, not opinions.
2 Create a class newspaper which can be displayed on the wall. (This can be done individually or in pairs or small groups.) Some suggestions:
   - a factual report of the trial and the judgement
   - interviews with people who have suffered from – or been

helped by – the activities of Antonio and Shylock
- an interview with Antonio's gaoler
- an interview with Jessica at Belmont
- Portia's story, told by herself, from her father's death to the judgement on Shylock
- a fashion page
- portraits of the main characters as you see them (You can find photographs in magazines to show the characteristics you are looking for.)
- an investigation into how Bassanio has managed to lose so much money in the past
- an account of the voyage to England by one of Antonio's captains
- a recipe page highlighting some of the spices Antonio trades in.

3 Read Antonio's farewell speech again and write what it would sound like in prose, in simple, modern English.

4 Bassanio and Gratiano have given away the rings which they promised they would never part with. They know that they are bound to get into trouble for this. Write an extra scene for the play in which they invent and rehearse their excuses.

Quiz

1 Who are examples of hard-heartedness?
2 What has Shylock sworn by?
3 Does a snake really sting?
4 Which kind of fruit drops earliest to the ground?
5 How can mercy be said to be '*twice blest*'?
6 How much money does Shylock say he would refuse? Do the sum!

Who is:

7 '*a stormy adversary, an inhuman wretch*'?
8 '*a learned doctor*'?
9 '*a tainted wether of the flock*'?
10 '*a Daniel come to judgement*'?
11 '*armed and well prepared*'?
12 '*not well*'?

At Belmont, Lorenzo and Jessica are enjoying the moonlight and being in love. They bring to mind stories of lovers in myth and legend.

1 It is a moonlit night with a soft breeze. Lorenzo remembers the story of how Troilus, still in Troy, longed for Cressida, then with the Greeks.

2 Jessica speaks of Thisbe. Pyramus and Thisbe were forbidden to marry. They arranged to meet, but Thisbe, arriving first, was frightened away by a lion. It tore and bloodied her scarf. Pyramus, finding this and assuming the worst, killed himself. Thisbe, finding his dead body, then killed herself.

3 Lorenzo's next thought is of Dido who, when her husband was murdered, escaped with his treasure. Granted land in Africa, she later fell in love with Aeneas.

4 Medea, for a while Jason's wife, made Jason's father Æson young again by boiling him in a cauldron with magic herbs she had gathered at night.

5 Lorenzo brings the stories of love up to the present and he and Jessica talk of their love and elopement.

Act five

Scene 1

Belmont

Enter LORENZO *and* JESSICA

LORENZO   The moon shines bright. In such a night as this,
              When the sweet wind did gently kiss the trees,
              And they did make no noise, in such a night
              Troilus methinks mounted the Trojan walls,
              And sighed his soul toward the Grecian tents
              Where Cressid lay that night.

JESSICA   In such a night
              Did Thisbe fearfully o'ertrip the dew,
              And saw the lion's shadow ere himself,
              And ran dismayed away.

LORENZO   In such a night
              Stood Dido with a willow in her hand   10
              Upon the wild sea banks, and waft her love
              To come again to Carthage.

JESSICA   In such a night
              Medea gathered the enchanted herbs
              That did renew old Æson.

LORENZO   In such a night
              Did Jessica steal from the wealthy Jew,
              And with an unthrift love did run from Venice,
              As far as Belmont.

JESSICA   In such a night
              Did young Lorenzo swear he loved her well,
              Stealing her soul with many vows of faith,
              And ne'er a true one.

LORENZO   In such a night   20

There is news of both Portia's and Bassanio's imminent arrival.

6 Stephano, a messenger from Portia, still telling of her religious activities, says she will soon be home.

6 >

7 Launcelot has heard that Bassanio will shortly return.

7 >

| | Did pretty Jessica, like a little shrew,
Slander her love, and he forgave it her. |
| JESSICA | I would out-night you, did no body come.
But hark, I hear the footing of a man. |

Enter STEPHANO

LORENZO	Who comes so fast in silence of the night?
STEPHANO	A friend.
LORENZO	A friend? What friend? Your name I pray you, friend?
STEPHANO	Stephano is my name, and I bring word My mistress will before the break of day Be here at Belmont; she doth stray about 30 By holy crosses where she kneels and prays For happy wedlock hours.
LORENZO	Who comes with her?
STEPHANO	None but a holy hermit and her maid. I pray you is my master yet returned?
LORENZO	He is not, nor we have not heard from him. But go we in I pray thee Jessica, And ceremoniously let us prepare Some welcome for the mistress of the house.

Enter LAUNCELOT

LAUNCELOT	Sola, sola! Wo ha ho! Sola, sola!
LORENZO	Who calls? 40
LAUNCELOT	Sola! Did you see Master Lorenzo? Master Lorenzo, sola, sola!
LORENZO	Leave holloaing man, here.
LAUNCELOT	Sola! Where, where?
LORENZO	Here.
LAUNCELOT	Tell him there's a post come from my master, with his horn full of good news: my master will be here ere morning. *[Exit*

Lorenzo and Jessica stay outside while music plays.
Lorenzo speaks of the power of music.

8 ▷

8 Stephano goes in to tell the servants to prepare for their mistress' and master's return and to order the group of musicians to play.

Become: suit, are fitting for
touches: playing, fingering the strings
floor of heaven: the night sky
patens: plates of silver or gold used at the communion service. Some editions read 'patterns' which makes equally good sense.
orb: star or planet
motion: the sun, moon and planets were thought to be in hollow globes, which, as they revolved, made harmonious sounds – 'the music of the spheres'
quiring: continually making music
cherubins: small angels
Such...souls: the same harmony exists in the souls of men
muddy vesture...it in: while the body still keeps the soul of every man imprisoned
we...it: '*it*' here is 'the harmony'
wake Diana: keep watch for their virgin mistress (Portia)

1 ▷

1 Lorenzo tells Jessica how, if animals suddenly hear music, they become quiet and docile.

LORENZO   Sweet soul, let's in, and there expect their coming.
            And yet no matter–why should we go in?   50
            My friend Stephano, signify I pray you
            Within the house, your mistress is at hand,
            And bring your music forth into the air.
                                                    [*Exit Stephano*
            How sweet the moonlight sleeps upon this bank.
            Here will we sit, and let the sounds of music
            Creep in our ears. Soft stillness and the night
            Become the touches of sweet harmony.
            Sit Jessica. Look how the floor of heaven
            Is thick inlaid with patens of bright gold.
            There's not the smallest orb which thou
                behold'st   60
            But in his motion like an angel sings,
            Still quiring to the young-eyed cherubins;
            Such harmony is in immortal souls,
            But whilst this muddy vesture of decay
            Doth grossly close it in, we cannot hear it.

            Enter Musicians

            Come ho, and wake Diana with a hymn,
            With sweetest touches pierce your mistress' ear,
            And draw her home with music.   [*Music*

JESSICA   I am never merry when I hear sweet music.

LORENZO   The reason is your spirits are attentive.   70
            For do but note a wild and wanton herd,
            Or race of youthful and unhandled colts,
            Fetching mad bounds, bellowing and neighing
                loud,
            Which is the hot condition of their blood;
            If they but hear perchance a trumpet sound,
            Or any air of music touch their ears,
            You shall perceive them make a mutual stand,
            Their savage eyes turned to a modest gaze
            By the sweet power of music. Therefore the poet

Lorenzo claims that a man with no musical sense is likely to be dull and treacherous. Portia and Nerissa approach the house, obviously content to be back.

2 >

---

2 Orpheus, in Greek myth, was able to charm with his music even inanimate objects and forces of nature.

3 A man who cannot appreciate music is not to be trusted.

3 >

4 Portia and Nerissa, returning, see the house lights from a distance.

4 >

5 Although the light seems bright now, it was formerly outshone by the moon.

5 >

6 The music sounds better than it does by day because the world is quiet – there are no rival sounds. Everything has its right time and place.

6 >

7 Portia calls out a greeting.

7 >

Did feign that Orpheus drew trees, stones, and
    floods;   80
Since nought so stockish, hard, and full of rage,
But music for the time doth change his nature.
The man that hath no music in himself,
Nor is not moved with concord of sweet sounds,
Is fit for treasons, stratagems, and spoils;
The motions of his spirit are dull as night,
And his affections dark as Erebus:
Let no such man be trusted. Mark the music.

Enter PORTIA *and* NERISSA

PORTIA   That light we see is burning in my hall.
How far that little candle throws his beams,   90
So shines a good deed in a naughty world.

NERISSA   When the moon shone we did not see the candle.

PORTIA   So doth the greater glory dim the less.
A substitute shines brightly as a king
Until a king be by, and then his state
Empties itself, as doth an inland brook
Into the main waters. Music, hark.

NERISSA   It is your music, madam, of the house.

PORTIA   Nothing is good I see without respect,
Methinks it sounds much sweeter than by day.   100

NERISSA   Silence bestows that virtue on it, madam.

PORTIA   The crow doth sing as sweetly as the lark
When neither is attended; and I think
The nightingale, if she should sing by day
When every goose is cackling, would be thought
No better a musician than the wren.
How many things by season seasoned are
To their right praise and true perfection.
Peace ho, the moon sleeps with Endymion,
And would not be awaked.

                                          [Music ceases

Portia and Nerissa are welcomed home and shortly afterwards they welcome their returning husbands and Antonio.

8 Portia still pretends that they have been praying for their husbands' safety and success.

9 Everyone is asked not to reveal the secret – that Portia and Nerissa have been away as long as their husbands.

10 The men are welcomed.

bound: Bassanio and Portia play on the word '*bound*'. Bassanio uses it to mean 'indebted' and 'close in friendship'. Portia repeats the meaning of 'indebted, obliged' and in the third use of the word suggests that Antonio had 'pledged' his life to Shylock and was also held 'bound' in jail. (See GLOSSARY: *Play on words, Pun* page 236)

LORENZO	That is the voice, 110
	Or I am much deceived, of Portia.
PORTIA	He knows me as the blind man knows the cuckoo–
	By the bad voice.
LORENZO	Dear lady welcome home.
PORTIA	We have been praying for our husbands' welfare,
	Which speed, we hope, the better for our words.
	Are they returned?
LORENZO	Madam, they are not yet;
	But there is come a messenger before
	To signify their coming.
PORTIA	Go in Nerissa;
	Give order to my servants that they take
	No note at all of our being absent hence– 120
	Nor you, Lorenzo–Jessica, nor you.
	[A tucket sounds
LORENZO	Your husband is at hand, I hear his trumpet.
	We are no tell-tales madam, fear you not.
PORTIA	This night methinks is but the daylight sick,
	It looks a little paler; 'tis a day,
	Such as the day is when the sun is hid.

Enter BASSANIO, ANTONIO, GRATIANO, *and their followers*

BASSANIO	We should hold day with the Antipodes,
	If you would walk in absence of the sun.
PORTIA	Let me give light, but let me not be light;
	For a light wife doth make a heavy husband, 130
	And never be Bassanio so for me.
	But God sort all. You are welcome home my lord.
BASSANIO	I thank you madam. Give welcome to my friend.
	This is the man, this is Antonio,
	To whom I am so infinitely bound.
PORTIA	You should in all sense be much bound to him,
	For as I hear he was much bound for you.

A quarrel starts between Gratiano and Nerissa over her ring. Portia joins in, saying she is sure Bassanio still has hers.

---

acquitted of: repaid
It: the welcome
Therefore...courtesy: So I will stop merely speaking words of welcome
gelt: gelded
paltry: insignificant, worthless
posy: inscription round the inside of a ring
cutler's poetry: doggerel verse, such as might be inscribed on a knife handle
leave: abandon, part with (the ring)
respective: careful of it
on's: on his
an if: if
scrubbed: stunted
prating: chattering, talkative
slightly: carelessly

ANTONIO	No more than I am well acquitted of.
PORTIA	Sir, you are very welcome to our house.
	It must appear in other ways than words, 140
	Therefore I scant this breathing courtesy.
GRATIANO	[*To Nerissa*] By yonder moon I swear you do me wrong,
	In faith I gave it to the judge's clerk.
	Would he were gelt that had it for my part,
	Since you do take it, love, so much at heart.
PORTIA	A quarrel ho, already? What's the matter?
GRATIANO	About a hoop of gold, a paltry ring
	That she did give me, whose posy was
	For all the world like cutler's poetry
	Upon a knife, 'Love me, and leave me not'. 150
NERISSA	What talk you of the posy or the value?
	You swore to me when I did give it you,
	That you would wear it till your hour of death,
	And that it should lie with you in your grave.
	Though not for me, yet for your vehement oaths,
	You should have been respective and have kept it.
	Gave it a judge's clerk? No, God's my judge,
	The clerk will ne'er wear hair on's face that had it.
GRATIANO	He will, an if he live to be a man.
NERISSA	Ay, if a woman live to be a man. 160
GRATIANO	Now by this hand I gave it to a youth,
	A kind of boy, a little scrubbed boy,
	No higher than thyself, the judge's clerk,
	A prating boy that begged it as a fee.
	I could not for my heart deny it him.
PORTIA	You were to blame, I must be plain with you,
	To part so slightly with your wife's first gift,
	A thing stuck on with oaths upon your finger,
	And riveted with faith unto your flesh.
	I gave my love a ring, and made him swear 170
	Never to part with it, and here he stands.

Bassanio realizes he is in a fix and Gratiano now unkindly gives him away. Portia threatens not to sleep with Bassanio until she sees the ring. Bassanio tries to explain.

Not that I hope: I hope not the one
void: empty
would conceive: could imagine
left: parted with
abate the strength…displeasure: not be so deeply offended by what I have done.
virtue: power

	I dare be sworn for him he would not leave it,
	Nor pluck it from his finger, for the wealth
	That the world masters. Now in faith Gratiano,
	You give your wife too unkind a cause of grief.
	And't were to me I should be mad at it.

BASSANIO [*Aside*] Why I were best to cut my left hand off,
And swear I lost the ring defending it.

GRATIANO My Lord Bassanio gave his ring away
Unto the judge that begged it, and indeed   180
Deserved it too. And then the boy his clerk
That took some pains in writing, he begged mine,
And neither man nor master would take aught
But the two rings.

PORTIA   What ring gave you, my lord?
Not that, I hope, which you received of me.

BASSANIO If I could add a lie unto a fault,
I would deny it; but you see my finger
Hath not the ring upon it, it is gone.

PORTIA Even so void is your false heart of truth.
By heaven I will ne'er come in your bed   190
Until I see the ring.

NERISSA   Nor I in yours
Till I again see mine.

BASSANIO   Sweet Portia,
If you did know to whom I gave the ring,
If you did know for whom I gave the ring,
And would conceive for what I gave the ring
And how unwillingly I left the ring,
When nought would be accepted but the ring,
You would abate the strength of your displeasure.

PORTIA If you had known the virtue of the ring,
Or half her worthiness that gave the ring,   200
Or your own honour to contain the ring,
You would not then have parted with the ring.
What man is there so much unreasonable,

Bassanio explains what happened. Portia and Nerissa swear that if these 'men' turn up they'll sleep with them. Antonio is embarrassed.

terms of zeal: enthusiasm, conviction
wanted the modesty: that would have lacked the restraint to go on demanding something kept as a symbol
civil doctor: doctor of civil law
suffered: allowed
uphold: save
beset with shame and courtesy: covered in shame and with a need to do the courteous thing
candles: stars
liberal: generous
Argus: a monster with a hundred eyes
mar...pen: both damage his pen (he is a clerk) and castrate him

If you had pleased to have defended it
With any terms of zeal, wanted the modesty
To urge the thing held as a ceremony?
Nerissa teaches me what to believe:
I'll die for't, but some woman had the ring.

BASSANIO   No by my honour madam, by my soul
No woman had it, but a civil doctor,   210
Which did refuse three thousand ducats of me,
And begged the ring, the which I did deny him,
And suffered him to go displeased away,
Even he that did uphold the very life
Of my dear friend. What should I say sweet lady?
I was enforced to send it after him.
I was beset with shame and courtesy;
My honour would not let ingratitude
So much besmear it. Pardon me good lady,
For by these blessed candles of the night,   220
Had you been there, I think you would have
        begged
The ring of me to give the worthy doctor.

PORTIA   Let not that doctor e'er come near my house.
Since he hath got the jewel that I loved,
And that which you did swear to keep for me,
I will become as liberal as you;
I'll not deny him anything I have,
No, not my body, nor my husband's bed.
Know him I shall, I am well sure of it.
Lie not a night from home. Watch me like
        Argus.   230
If you do not, if I be left alone,
Now by mine honour, which is yet mine own,
I'll have that doctor for my bedfellow.

NERISSA   And I his clerk. Therefore be well advised
How you do leave me to mine own protection.

GRATIANO   Well do you so. Let me not take him then,
For if I do, I'll mar the young clerk's pen.

Bassanio swears he will never again break faith with
Portia. Antonio guarantees his word and Portia gives him
the same ring again. They explain.

In both my eyes...self: Bassanio sees himself reflected in both
of Portia's eyes. She teases him by suggesting that this
makes him two-faced, so that '*And there's an oath of credit*' is
heavily ironic. (See GLOSSARY: *Irony*, page 235)

of credit: to be believed

Had quite miscarried: would have been completely lost

My...forfeit: my soul as the penalty

advisedly: consciously

surety: guarantor. Antonio will guarantee that Bassanio will
keep his promise.

In lieu of: in return for

Why this is like...it?: Portia and Nerissa each claim to have
slept with the 'man' to whom her ring was given. Gratiano
jokingly states that the women have thus cheated on them
before they could possibly have deserved such treatment –
just as, he says, the roads are mended in summer before
winter has put them into a bad state of repair.

grossly: coarsely

amazed: bewildered

ANTONIO	I am the unhappy subject of these quarrels.
PORTIA	Sir, grieve not you, you are welcome notwithstanding.
BASSANIO	Portia, forgive me this enforced wrong, 240 And in the hearing of these many friends I swear to thee, even by thine own fair eyes Wherein I see myself–
PORTIA	Mark you but that? In both my eyes he doubly sees himself, In each eye, one–swear by your double self, And there's an oath of credit.
BASSANIO	Nay, but hear me. Pardon this fault, and by my soul I swear I never more will break an oath with thee.
ANTONIO	I once did lend my body for his wealth, Which but for him that had your husband's ring 250 Had quite miscarried. I dare be bound again, My soul upon the forfeit, that your lord Will never more break faith advisedly.
PORTIA	Then you shall be his surety. Give him this, And bid him keep it better than the other.
ANTONIO	Here Lord Bassanio, swear to keep this ring.
BASSANIO	By heaven it is the same I gave the doctor.
PORTIA	I had it of him. Pardon me Bassanio, For by this ring the doctor lay with me.
NERISSA	And pardon me my gentle Gratiano, 260 For that same scrubbed boy the doctor's clerk, In lieu of this last night did lie with me.
GRATIANO	Why this is like the mending of highways In summer where the ways are fair enough. What, are we cuckolds ere we have deserved it?
PORTIA	Speak not so grossly. You are all amazed. Here is a letter, read it at your leisure–

There is a letter for Antonio about his ships, and a deed of gift for Lorenzo and Jessica.

---

even but now: only just a moment ago
life and living: '*life*' because of the business in court, and
  '*living*' because of the news that he is still in business
road: safe anchorage
manna: the food which God sent from heaven to feed the
  Israelites in the desert
you...full: you haven't yet heard enough detail about these
  events
charge...inter'gatories: you can take statements from us

It comes from Padua from Bellario—
There you shall find that Portia was the doctor,
Nerissa there her clerk. Lorenzo here   270
Shall witness I set forth as soon as you,
And even but now returned. I have not yet
Entered my house. Antonio you are welcome,
And I have better news in store for you
Than you expect. Unseal this letter soon,
There you shall find three of your argosies
Are richly come to harbour suddenly.
You shall not know by what strange accident
I chanced on this letter.

ANTONIO   I am dumb.

BASSANIO   Were you the doctor, and I knew you not?   280

GRATIANO   Were you the clerk that is to make me cuckold?

NERISSA   Ay but the clerk that never means to do it,
Unless he live until he be a man.

BASSANIO   Sweet doctor, you shall be my bedfellow.
When I am absent, then lie with my wife.

ANTONIO   Sweet lady, you have given me life and living;
For here I read for certain that my ships
Are safely come to road.

PORTIA   How now Lorenzo?
My clerk hath some good comforts too for you.

NERISSA   Ay, and I'll give them him without a fee.   290
There do I give to you and Jessica
From the rich Jew, a special deed of gift
After his death, of all he dies possessed of.

LORENZO   Fair ladies, you drop manna in the way
Of starved people.

PORTIA   It is almost morning,
And yet I am sure you are not satisfied
Of these events at full. Let us go in,
And charge us there upon inter'gatories,
And we will answer all things faithfully.

Gratiano offers Nerissa the choice of going to bed for the remaining two hours of the night. He will always be sure to keep her ring safely.

stay: wait
were...come: if it were already day
That I were: so that I could be
I'll...as: nothing will concern me more than

 # CTIVITIES

Keeping track

1 Why do Lorenzo and Jessica remind each other of the stories of classical lovers?
2 What news interrupts this romantic scene?
3 How does the beginning of Act 5 compare with what we know of the beginning of Lorenzo's and Jessica's marriage?
4 What are Portia's feelings as she approaches her house?
5 What is the first row to break out?
6 How do Gratiano and Bassanio try to justify parting with the rings?
7 How can the newly-weds threaten to sleep with the men who took their rings – and mean it?
8 What effect do the quarrels have on Antonio?
9 Portia and Nerissa have the rings. What does this prove to Antonio, Gratiano and Bassanio?
10 How do Antonio, Lorenzo and Jessica benefit from news that Portia brings?

Discussion

1 Was Bassanio right or wrong in giving away the ring?
2 Which should be more important, a relationship with friends or with husband/wife, boyfriend/girlfriend?
3 Do you think that by the end of the play Bassanio has a

GRATIANO　　　Let it be so. The first inter'gatory　　　300
　　　　　　　That my Nerissa shall be sworn on is,
　　　　　　　Whether till the next night she had rather stay,
　　　　　　　Or go to bed now, being two hours to day.
　　　　　　　But were the day come, I should wish it dark
　　　　　　　That I were couching with the doctor's clerk.
　　　　　　　Well, while I live I'll fear no other thing
　　　　　　　So sore, as keeping safe Nerissa's ring.　　　[*Exeunt*

different opinion of Portia from the one he held at the
beginning?

4 Does the play have a 'happy ending'?

Drama

1 In pairs:
Either:
- You invite your boyfriend/girlfriend to the cinema.
- He/she is already going out with a group of friends.
- Improvise the scene in which you complain that he/she never has time for you.

Or:
- You were given a gold watch by your grandmother.
- It has real value and it has sentimental value for her.
- It has simply disappeared, the way things do.
- Your grandmother is coming to stay and will expect to see you wearing it.
- Improvise the scene in which you and a friend desperately try to think of excuses to explain where it is.

2 The most amusing moment in the final scene is when Portia assures Gratiano that her lover would never part with the ring she gave him (Act 5 scene 1 lines 170–174).
- Use FORUM THEATRE (see page 210) to explore this.

- What does Gratiano think?
- What is Bassanio doing?

Character

1 Did Lorenzo and Jessica elope because Jessica wanted to escape from Shylock and Lorenzo wanted her money, or are they really in love?

2 It may seem difficult to judge character when Portia and Nerissa are playing a part for much of this scene – but what do we learn about them? Look both at their homecoming and at the joke they are playing on the men.

3 Bassanio and Gratiano hardly know their wives at all. Bearing this in mind, how do they take the trick that was played on them?

4 What do you think of Antonio now? How important does he seem in Act 5?

5 Complete your CHARACTER LOGS.

Close study

1 The comedy in Act 5 is in the situation, in the words, and in the way the words are delivered.
   - Describe the situation.
   - Find lines which express the comedy. You may well be looking for exaggerated statements.
   - Find lines which look ordinary but which the actor can make comic by looks and tone of voice.

2 We have looked before at the use of repetition and rhyme in the play.
   - Look at lines 192–208.
   - What do you notice about them?
   - What effect do you think these devices have
     a on the characters in the scene?
     b on the audience?
   - If you were the actors, how would you deliver these two speeches? Try it out in pairs.

3 The beginning of Act 5 is romantic and serene and in

particular Lorenzo's speech (lines 54–65) is in sharp contrast to the language of the previous scene. Look back through the play and find other places where Shakespeare has lightened the drama with comedy or with a change of pace. Make a note of these.

Writing

1 It is ten years after the events of the play. Take one of the characters and write, from their point of view, what has happened to them and how the events of ten years ago shaped their lives.
2 What happens to Shylock at the end of the play? Write a balanced judgement of his character. Give your writing the title 'Shylock: Villain or Victim?'

Quiz

This wordsquare contains words of key importance in the play. They run horizontally, vertically, from bottom to top, and back to front, but not diagonally.

If you find 25 you're doing well, but there may be a couple more!

```
L D I S G U I S E A B F D
O U C P M N O P Y G O L D
V K S W Z E R I C H T E Q
E E Q D U C A T S E Z S W
Z T U S U R Y Y X I P H W
S H I P S M M J E R R F R
T R J K D O G L R E O W E
E I B R P N N O E S D T C
K F O R F E I T V S I U K
S T N Q S Y C R E M G L S
A G D E B T S V N W A E X
C H S I L V E R G X L A W
I N T E R E S T E H J D I
```

Explorations

Keeping track

When you are studying a play, one of the most difficult things to do is to keep track of all the ideas and information you gain as you work on it scene by scene. It is important to keep a note of what you do. Two good ways of organizing your work are to keep a SCENE LOG and a CHARACTER LOG.

Scene log

As you work on each scene, make a list of the basic information about it:
• when and where it takes place
◆ the characters in it
• what happens.
Then add any thoughts and comments you want to remember. You could use the layout illustrated opposite – or you may prefer to make up your own.

Character log

At the same time, you can keep a log for each of the main characters. Use this to record what you find out about the character in every scene he or she appears:
• key points about the character
• your reasons for choosing these
• the numbers of important lines
• short quotations to back up the key points.
Again there is a layout opposite, but you may prefer your own approach.

Scene log

Act/scene	Time/place	Characters	Action	Comments
1/2	Belmont. Portia's house.	Portia, Nerissa	Portia and Nerissa discuss the contest of the caskets, by which Portia's husband must be chosen. Six young men leave. The Prince of Morocco will be next.	Portia's father has tried to protect her from fortune hunters. She is unhappy that she has no choice.

Character log

Character: Portia

Act/scene	Key points	Reasons	Key lines	Short quotations
1/2	She feels low	She has to follow her dead father's method of choosing her husband.	22–26	I cannot choose one, nor refuse none.
	She has a sense of humour	She gives a short, witty portrait of each of her suitors	36–90	God made him, and therefore let him pass for a man.

Drama activities

Most of these activities can be done in small groups or by the class as a whole. They work by slowing down the action of the play and helping you focus on a small section of it – so that you can think more deeply about characters, plot and themes.

Hotseating

Hotseating means putting one of the characters 'under the microscope' at a particular point in the play. This is how it works:

1 Begin by choosing a particular character and a particular moment in the play. For example, you might choose Antonio at the moment when he agrees to sign the bond for a pound of his flesh (Act 1 scene 3 line 149).

2 One person (student or teacher) is selected to be the chosen character.

3 That person sits 'in the hotseat', with the rest of the group arranged round in a semi-circle, or a circle.

4 The rest then ask questions about how the character feels, why s/he has acted in that way, and so on. Try to keep the questions going and not to give the person in the hotseat too much time to think.

Variations

1 The questioners themselves take on roles. (In the example above they could be Antonio's other friends.)

2 Characters can be hotseated at a series of key moments in a scene to see how their opinions and attitudes change.

3 The questioners can take different attitudes to the character, for example:
   • aggressive
   • pleading
   • disbelieving.

Freeze!

It is very useful to be able to 'stop the action' and concentrate on a single moment in the play. You can do this in a number of ways.

Photographs

Imagine that someone has taken a photograph of a particular moment, or that – as if it were a film or video – the action has been frozen. Once you have chosen the moment, you can work in a number of different ways:

- Act that part of the scene and then 'Freeze!' – you will probably find it easier if you have a 'director' standing outside the scene to shout 'Freeze!'
- Discuss what the photograph should look like and then arrange yourselves into the photograph.
- One at a time place yourselves in the photograph; each person 'entering' it must take notice of what is there already.
- Once you have arranged the photograph, take it in turns to come out of it and comment on it, with suggestions for improvements.

There are a number of ways in which you can develop your photograph:

- Each person takes it in turn to speak his/her thoughts at that moment in the scene.
- The photograph is given a caption.
- Some members of the group do not take part in the photograph. Instead they provide a sound track of speech or sound effects, or both.

Statues/Paintings

Make a statue or a painting like this:

1 Select a moment in the play, or a title from the play, for example, 'Why all the boys in Venice follow him,
   Crying, his stones, his daughter and his ducats' (Act 2 scene 8).
2 Choose one member of the group to be the sculptor/painter. That person then arranges the rest of the group, one at a time to make the statue or painting.

Statues and paintings are different from photographs in two important ways:
- they are made up by an 'artist' and tell us about the artist's view of the person or event;
- if they talk, they tell us about what they can 'see', for example, how people react when they see the statue or painting for the first time.

Forum theatre

In FORUM THEATRE, one or two people take on roles and the rest of the group are 'directors'. It works like this:

1 Select a moment in the play. (For example, the moment when the gaoler brings Antonio out of prison to meet Shylock in Act 3 scene 3.)
2 Select members of the group to be Antonio, Shylock and the gaoler.
3 Organize your working area, so that everyone knows where the other characters are, where characters make entrances and exits, and so on.
4 Begin by asking Antonio, Shylock and the gaoler to offer their own first thoughts about position, gesture, and movement.
5 The directors then experiment with different ways of presenting that moment. They can:
- ask Antonio, Shylock and the gaoler to take up particular positions, use particular gestures, move in certain ways
- ask them to speak in a particular way
- discuss with them how they might move or speak and why – for example, to communicate a certain set of thoughts and feelings.
6 The short sequence can be repeated a number of times, until the directors have used up all their ideas about their interpretation.

Shakespeare's language

It is easy to look at the text of this play and say to yourself, 'I'm never going to understand that!' But it is important not to be put off. Remember that there are two reasons why Shakespeare's language may seem strange at first.

1   He was writing four hundred years ago and the English language has changed over the centuries.
2   He wrote mainly in verse. As a result he sometimes changed the order of words to make them fit the verse form, and he used a large number of 'tricks of the trade': figures of speech and other verse techniques (which are listed in the GLOSSARY, page 234).

Language change

This can cause three main kinds of problem:

Grammar

Since the end of the sixteenth century there have been some changes in English grammar. Some examples:

1   *Thee, thou, thy*, and the verb forms that go with them are used alongside *you, your*.

Jessica:	'*Who are you? Tell me for more certainty,*
	Albeit I swear that I do know your tongue.'
Lorenzo:	'*Lorenzo and thy love.*'

Thou is used from master to servant:

Bassanio:	'*I know thee well, thou hast obtained thy suit.*
	Shylock thy master spoke with me this day
	And hath preferred thee …'

How do you interpret this use?

Gratiano:	'*You must not deny me, I must go with you to*
	Belmont.'
Bassanio:	'*Why then you must. But hear thee Gratiano,*
	Thou art too wild, too rude and bold of voice,'

2   Words contract (shorten) in different ways. For example: *'tis* rather than *it's*; *ne'er* for *never*.
3   Some of the 'little words' are different. For example: *an* for *if*, *ay* for *yes*, *twain* for *two*.

Words that have changed their meaning

Sometimes you will come across words that you think you know, but discover that they don't mean what you expect them to mean. For example:

'*naughty*' (Act 3 scene 3 line 9) meant 'wicked' or 'worthless' in Shakespeare's day. Now it means 'disobedient' or 'badly-behaved'. In the same line '*fond*' now suggests affection. Then it meant 'foolish'.

Words that have gone out of use

These are the most obvious and most frequent causes of difficulty. Shakespeare had – and used – a huge vocabulary. He loved using words, and pushing them to their limits. So you will come across many words you have not met before. They are usually explained in the notes.

The language of the play

Most of *The Merchant of Venice* is in blank verse but parts are in prose and short sections are in rhymed verse.

Blank verse

The main part of the play is written in lines of ten syllables with a repeated pattern of weak and strong 'beats':

'*Thou **art** too **wild**, too **rude** and **bold** of **voice***'

(ti **tum** ti **tum** ti **tum** ti **tum** ti **tum**)

Had Shakespeare given every line exactly the same rhythm the play would soon become very monotonous, so he varies the rhythm in a number of ways. Sometimes lines are not exactly ten syllables long or are divided between two or more characters. Often he just changes the pattern of weak and strong beats slightly:

'***Why** doth the **Jew pause? Take** thy **forfeiture***'

(**tum** ti ti **tum tum tum** ti **tum** ti **tum**)

But this line, at a turning point in the play, also has one extra strong beat, and a deliberate pause for effect in the middle of the line, called the caesura (see GLOSSARY).

He also expected the actors to speak his lines in a natural manner, not pausing at the end of each line unless the sense of the words made it necessary.

Say the following lines twice, first pausing at the end of each line and the second time pausing only where there is a comma, semi-colon or full stop:

Portia: '*I pray you tarry, pause a day or two*
Before you hazard, for in choosing wrong
I lose your company; therefore forbear awhile.
There's something tells me – but it is not love –
I would not lose you, and you know yourself
Hate counsels not in such a quality.'

Portia is in love with Bassanio. She must not say so, but she can't help it. She wants him to make the choice that will win her, but she is afraid he will fail and she will lose him for ever.

- How does the writing help to express these opposing feelings? Look at repetition and contradiction.
- How does the punctuation help to get this confusion across?
- Do you think this would be better as prose – or does the verse, even when the beat isn't made obvious, give it a shape it needs?

When the ten-syllable lines do not rhyme they are known as *blank verse*.

Rhymed verse

Sometimes Shakespeare uses a pattern of rhymed lines. It may be just two successive lines, known as a heroic couplet:

Portia: '*How all the other passions fleet to air,*
As doubtful thoughts, and rash-embraced despair'

Such couplets are often used to round off a scene. Sometimes characters who exit one after the other each have a rhyming couplet.

Shylock: '*Fast bind, fast find,*
A proverb never stale in thrifty mind.'   [Exit]

Jessica: '*Farewell, and if my fortune be not crossed,*
I have a father, you a daughter lost.'   [Exit]

Sometimes the pattern of rhyme varies. When Bassanio, just married, leaves on his apparently hopeless mission to free

Antonio, the leave-taking is more ceremonious:

Bassanio: *'Since I have your good leave to go away,*
I will make haste; but till I come again,
No bed shall e'er be guilty of my stay,
Nor rest be interposer 'twixt us twain.'

The need for ceremony and a 'rounded' end to the situation produces rhymed verses for the scrolls which the losers – and the winner – find in the three caskets.

Prose

Much of the play is written in prose – ordinary sentences. If you look at the play as a whole, you will see that prose is used for certain characters and situations. Look, for example, at these sections:

Act 2 scene 2 (whole scene)

Act 3 scene 1 (whole scene)

Why do you think prose is used for these characters and situations?

Themes

The title

If you mention Shakespeare's play *The Merchant of Venice* to people who have read it, seen it or heard about it, the character they remember is Shylock the moneylender, not Antonio, the merchant of the title.

- If this is true of your impression of the play, can you suggest why this is?
- Look again at what we learn about the two men, and how we learn it. How often does Antonio address us directly about his feelings? What about Shylock?
- Is there a speech of Antonio's to match the way Shylock speaks in Act 3 scene 1 lines 54–69?
- Our first encounters with Shylock encourage us to regard Shylock as a monster. Do your feelings about him change at all at the end of the trial scene?
- Do you think the title 'The Jew of Venice', which has sometimes been used for this play, is more suitable?
- Could you create a new title featuring another central character?
- Do we, in spite of ourselves, look on characters who are in conflict with society as more interesting than characters who behave as society thinks they should?
- Argue this last point by giving examples from your own reading or viewing.

Stereotypes and prejudice

Portia jokingly uses stereotyping when she dismisses the thought of marrying any of the first six young men who think of trying their luck with the caskets. This doesn't seem too serious; we all have our own ideas on what Frenchmen, Germans, Italians, Australians are like, usually based on far less evidence than Portia had. They have their theories about the British too.

- People on the mainland of Europe think we live constantly shrouded in mist. Is this true?
- The French think we are terrible cooks. Do you know some good ones?
- People in other European countries think we can't, or won't, learn their language. Is this fair?
- Because we live on an island, in a cool climate, we have the reputation for being cold, unfriendly and inhospitable. Are we?

It seems as though people need a simple 'filing system' to start with: some means of classifying other people. This is probably all right as long as we are prepared to modify it when we meet real people who are different from the stereotype. If we can't do this, then we can become set in our attitude of mind, and prejudice sets in. Prejudice is never the joke that stereotyping can be. It becomes obsessive and dangerous. As we saw in the INTRODUCTION (pages xvi to xviii), prejudice against the Jews has been widespread for centuries.

Shylock

The figure of Shylock is in many ways much more difficult for us to deal with today than for Shakespeare's audience. We are living after Hitler's attempt to wipe out the Jewish race. People in Shakespeare's day were unlikely to have met Jews who had not converted to Christianity – they had already been banned from England for three hundred years.

It is important to remember that a writer often creates characters who hold very different opinions from those of the writer himself. Antonio and many of his friends are antisemitic, but in places Shakespeare lets Shylock speak from the heart and we suddenly see him as a human being, not an alien stereotype.

1 Find the scenes and speeches where Shakespeare does this, and make a note of them, backed up with short quotations.
2 Look carefully at Act 1 scene 3. Some critics suggest that when Shylock offers to lend money without interest, he really means it kindly. What do you think?

3 Look at Act 3 scene 1. Shylock has been struck down by the double blow of losing his daughter and his money. What is more, he has lost Jessica to a Christian. Look for suggestions of sorrow and loneliness and the feelings he had for his dead wife.

4 When Shylock is sentenced, towards the end of Act 4 scene 1, we again feel pity for him. Can you explain why this is such an achievement on Shakespeare's part?

5 One of the elements in his sentence is that he must convert to Christianity. In Shakespeare's time this would not seem terrible, although it does to us today. His audience would consider that he was being offered salvation. How does Shakespeare show us that Shylock is completely crushed?

6 Some critics who have written about this play have suggested that the character of Shylock 'took over'. Shakespeare was writing a comedy, after all. When he stopped treating Shylock purely as a villain, an ogre, a wicked usurer, the comedy became a tragi-comedy. Why do you think Shylock does not appear at all in Act 5? Do you feel that the Shylock story is finished satisfactorily?

Writing

1 There is a very strong argument to support the theory that Shylock does not have a fair trial. Imagine that you are given the job of being his lawyer. What evidence would you bring in his defence?

Look carefully at Act 1 scene 3 where he suggests the bond with Antonio and at Act 3 scene 1 where he loses his daughter to a Christian and realizes at the same time that she is a thief.
Either:
Make the notes that you might use in his defence in court.
Or:
Write a closing speech which might persuade the Duke to be more merciful.

2 Some directors of *The Merchant of Venice* in the nineteenth century made their production of the play end at Shylock's final exit. Write one paragraph which argues that this could be a good idea, and another pointing out what you would miss.

Money

Both Antonio and Shylock are in the business of making money. Both are regarded as rich.

- How much money do you consider a person needs?
- Does having more than enough money make you happy?
- Have their riches made Antonio and Shylock happy?

Other characters in the play are also very interested in getting money – the money which the two female characters own or can acquire.

- Portia's father was concerned that her fortune would attract men with dubious motives. Was he right?
- What leads us to think at first that Bassanio too has the wrong attitude?
- He doesn't in the end use Portia's money to pay his debt to Antonio. Why not?
- Whose money is Lorenzo relying on? How does he get it?
- Who are shown to be the generous characters in the play?

Usury

In Shakespeare's day usury was very much frowned on, as being against 'the law of nations, the law of nature and the law of God.' Trade was acceptable because there was an element of adventure and of risk. However, then as now, in London as in Venice, people in business needed loans to extend their business, and as moneylending was one of the few businesses that Jews were allowed to operate, moneylenders were often Jews. The interest paid was resented and so was the wealth of the Jews.

- How do we regard borrowing nowadays?
- Make a list of the different kinds of borrowing that we have today.
- Research this topic by asking people what they think about borrowing, and by collecting advertisements persuading you to borrow money or take goods on credit.
- Is there such a thing as a fair rate of interest? What should it depend on?
- What does the phrase 'loan shark' tell you about our attitude

to moneylenders who charge a high rate of interest?

1 Use your researches to plan a television programme designed to show young people in a lively way the pros and cons of borrowing and of credit purchases. Focus on purchases which people of your own age might want to make.
Either:
Present the plan of the programme in the form of a storyboard.
Or:
Write a short 'blurb' for the programme you have planned, to appear in a teenage magazine or a television guide. It should make people of your age want to watch it.

2 Create a collage poster entitled 'Money'. You can choose your approach.

- You may want to illustrate the scenes from the play where money is important.
- You may prefer to make it much more general and include, for instance, some of your research material, and magazine and newspaper pictures of wealth and poverty, advertisements for football pools, lists of stocks and shares, expensive clothes, cars, etc.
- In the more general version of the poster you may like to make clear your attitude to the implications of international wealth and poverty.

Women

When Portia says in Act 1 scene 2, '*I may neither choose whom I would, nor refuse whom I dislike*' she is expressing the feelings of women down the ages, whose husbands have been chosen for them by their family on the grounds of wealth, social class, religion or race. Many of Shakespeare's plays exploit this conflict as a source of comedy or tragedy.

- We do not get the impression here that the situation is going to end in tragedy. Why not?
- After Portia has humorously run through the list of her would-be suitors' faults, she suddenly realizes the advantage to her of her father's decision. Look at Act 1 scene 2 lines 100–110 and

explain this benefit in your own words.
- Work through the scenes in which Portia appears. How does she hide her very real distress?
- She has to play a part when she doesn't like the suitors – and when she does. Find short quotations which express both these roles.
- Portia is beautiful, rich, intelligent and resourceful. Which of these assets would you say is the most important to the plot of the play?
- Portia rushes off on a daring impulse to rescue Antonio. Jessica runs away from her father to marry a Christian. Nerissa agrees to marry on the shortest possible acquaintance. Find a word or phrase to describe each of these women.

Fairytale elements

The story of the three caskets has many of the elements of a fairytale: Portia is the beautiful princess under a spell (the conditions laid down in her father's will); she is afraid she will be forced to marry a man she does not love; the least likely suitor (he is a commoner, not one of the princes) wins her; it has a happy ending.

1 Re-read the three caskets story and, in note form, write a short summary of it, making sure that you understand why the Prince of Morocco and the Prince of Arragon make the choice they do.
2 It is not until Act 2 scene 9 that we learn the detail of the three promises the suitors must make on oath. If you were telling the story would there be a better place for it?
Either:
Write a version of this story for a young child who likes fairytales, starting 'Once upon a time...'
Or:
Write a script for a puppet or glove-puppet play.

Do the writing on your own, but when you have finished, exchange what you have written with a partner. Criticize each other's work constructively. The storyline may not be clear enough or the sentences may be too long or some words too difficult for your audience. Make any alterations you agree on. Try out the story or the script on a young child you know.

Comedy or tragedy?

1 The commonly accepted definition of a Shakespearean comedy is a play that ends happily. However, although Shakespeare's comedies end happily on the surface, Shakespeare also leaves his audiences questioning whether the happy ending is real. If you were able to look beyond the end of the play, you might finds reasons to doubt whether the characters you have lived with through the play could be 'happy ever after'.
   - Which characters do you think might live happily after the end of the play?
   - Which characters might not?
   - Give reasons for your answers.

2 Throughout the play there are always possibilities that some happy events will become tragic and some tragic events will end happily.
   - Shakespeare will always give you indications of what you may expect. He won't spoil the story, of course, but by the language he uses, by what we have come to predict of the characters' behaviour, we are prepared, almost without realizing it, for what will happen.
   - Using two broad columns, one headed 'Situation' and the other 'Working out', examine the situations in *The Merchant of Venice* and the possibilities for tragedy or a happy outcome for each.

3 The clown was a character in most of Shakespeare's plays, whether comedies or tragedies. In a royal court or a great household he was the court jester, employed to entertain, to sing and to joke. He was also called 'the fool' or 'the patch', and originated in medieval morality plays as 'the Vice'. He often wore a multi-coloured costume.
   - As with the Vice, one of the clown's roles was to create mischief. Give examples of this from Launcelot's scene with his father (Act 2 scene 2). In line 62 Launcelot tells Old Gobbo that his son is dead. What effect does this have on

the blind old man? Do you think this is what Launcelot intended? Is it comic?

- Another of the clown's functions was to act as a link between the rather exotic world of the play and the world the audience knew. How does Launcelot do this?
- He was often the country boy come to town, or the idle servant. Find indications that Launcelot was both. Back these up with quotations if you can.
- It was sometimes difficult to tell whether the fool was stupid, or was hiding his cleverness by 'fooling'. What is your judgement of Launcelot?
- This last point was easier to decide in Shakespeare's day because the fool's part was written for a specific actor in the company. He would have many of the talents of a stand-up comic today. Which real comedian (man or woman) would you like to cast as Launcelot?
- The fool's part is almost always in prose. One reason is that it was easier for him to improvise within a prose speech. Looking back over the previous points can you think of other reasons? When does Launcelot break into rhyme?

The setting and the mood

Belmont and Venice

The action of the play takes place in Venice and at Belmont, Portia's country estate.

Venice is the city, the commercial centre, where deals are struck, where the talk is all of making and spending money, or making it grow. Ships are constantly being prepared for voyages to all parts of the world and ships are arriving to trade with the Venetians and add to their prosperity.

Belmont is distant from all this bustle. The talk here is of suitors, of love, and of a loving father's care for his daughter. Portia's mansion is set in parkland and Portia's money was made a long time ago. She is rich without having to make any effort. Others would like a share of her wealth, however, and here is the link between Venice and Belmont.

- Who are the travellers to Belmont in Acts 1 and 2? Why do they go there?
- Who go to Belmont in Act 3? What is their reason?
- In Act 4 Portia and Nerissa arrive in Venice. Why have they come?
- In Act 5 there is a visitor to Belmont who has not been there before. Who is he?

We soon learn what to expect of the scenes which take place in Venice and those which take place at Belmont.

- What differences between the two have you noticed?
- There is a great difference in atmosphere between Act 4, where all the action is in Venice, and Act 5 which takes place entirely at Belmont. How does the writing at the beginning of Act 5 help to show this contrast? Look at what it is about, as well as how it is written.
- Not quite all the problems for Bassanio, Gratiano and Antonio are solved by the beginning of Act 5. They could be serious. How does Shakespeare deal with them?

Ships and the sea

There is a mention in the play of a gondola, and of the ferry – both important forms of transport in Venice. But in the very first scene Shakespeare gives us a wider view which will be important both as background and as a central element in the plot throughout the play. Salerio and Solanio, trying to find a reason for Antonio's sad mood, paint a vivid picture of the dangers of wind and tide to sailing ships.

1 Make a note of these references to ships in the play. Use two broad columns. In the left-hand column make a list of the act and scene references given below. In the right-hand column write a short explanation of the importance of each reference, with a short quotation to fix it in your mind. You will find four of these references illustrated with drawings in this edition.
Act 1 scene 1; Act 1 scene 3; Act 2 scene 6; (also Act 2 scene 6 Bassanio sails for Belmont); (Act 2 scene 8 Shylock thought Jessica might be on Bassanio's ship); Act 2 scene 8; Act 3 scene 1; (Act 3 scene 1, Shylock is informed); Act 3 scene 2;

Act 5 scene 1.

2 Here are some points to consider for your second column. Does your reference:
- help to suggest the mood of characters or scene?
- help to fix Shylock's decision to be revenged?
- show the importance of rumour when communications are slow?
- give us a 'window on the world', taking us away from Venice and Belmont?
- show us a contrast – Shylock's means of earning a living is taken away from him at the trial; Antonio's is returned to him at the end of the play?
- help to demonstrate the risk and excitement of Antonio's 'ventures' contrasted with Shylock's usury, of which the Elizabethans disapproved?
- give Venetians the chance of a good gossip?
- show just how far ships travelled to do trade in the sixteenth century?
- tell us what the trading ships brought back from the east?
- keep reminding us just what Antonio is risking for his friend Bassanio?
- keep telling us how very important Venice is?
- show how one person's bad luck can be another's good luck?

The caskets

The attraction of gold and silver to men who are fortune-hunting is obvious and Portia's father certainly meant to discourage them. But each casket also carries an inscription.
- Look up and copy out the inscription for each casket (Act 2 scene 7)
- What difference do you notice in the verbs used for the silver and the gold, and those used for the lead?
- If 'me' is not gold, silver or lead, but Portia, do the inscriptions seem more significant?
- What is Portia's father saying about a happy marriage? Is taking or giving more important?

- Does Portia's free and willing gift of herself and everything she has to the man she loves, now make more sense?
- Do you think, by the end of the play, that Bassanio, who started out as a 'taker', is beginning to learn from her example?

Character activities

One of the most important things to do when studying a play is to get to know the characters really well. Keeping CHARACTER LOGS as you work through the play will give you plenty of raw material but it is also important to gain a picture of each character as a whole. The activities in this section will help you to do this.

Interpretation

As in real life, the characters in a play will only reveal themselves gradually. You may find that some characters always react as you expect them to after a first meeting. Other characters will be more complex, for example:

Bassanio

- Bassanio, who originally comes on with Lorenzo and Gratiano, obviously finds it difficult to put up with the latter's excessive talkativeness. He says: '*Gratiano speaks an infinite deal of nothing*' and he and Antonio very soon change the subject.
- Later we find Gratiano asking his friend, Bassanio, to take him to Belmont with him. Bassanio, as we know, sets a great deal of importance on this trip. He gives Gratiano a fairly severe lecture about his behaviour and gets a promise from him that he will behave properly.
- This is almost immediately followed by Bassanio's admission that he expects Gratiano to be the life and soul of the party that evening.

It is important that when you write up your CHARACTER LOGS you are prepared to let the characters have the same kind of inconsistencies that you meet with yourself. If they turn out to be unpredictable, don't just think you must have got it wrong before. As long as you can back your statements on character with a quotation you have understood, you will be right.

Minor characters

If you start with a character study of a relatively minor character, it is quicker to find the evidence you need. You will then find it easier to tackle the more complex characters, using the same method. Here is an example of questions you might answer to build up a log for a minor character:

Gratiano

Begin by asking yourself:

- When does he first appear?
- Is his first speech likely to make Antonio feel better or worse?
- What does this answer show you about him?
- If you've just claimed that someone doesn't look well, is it a good idea to nag them with a long speech?
- What does Gratiano say or imply about himself?

Once you have the beginnings of a list of characteristics, make sure you have the evidence for them by finding a short quotation for each. Locate each quotation by adding an act, scene, and line reference.

If you make a habit of noting down these details for every quotation you might wish to use, you will find it very useful when planning essays or preparing for an examination.

Gratiano appears again in Act 2 scenes 2, 4, 6; Act 3 scene 2; Act 4 scenes 1, 2 and Act 5. Do you find any change in his character in the course of the play?

Major characters

Obviously there is much more information given about the main characters of the play. They say more; their actions are more central to the plot; more people react to them; they shape the play.

This doesn't necessarily mean, however, that they are any more 'noble' or any nearer perfection than the lesser characters. Nor does it mean that things are necessarily any easier for them. There are characteristics which do not appear in words. Look at two examples:

Portia
- As the only daughter of a rich father in the sixteenth century Portia will almost certainly have had the best tutors available in every subject where she showed any talent. Her conversation is full of evidence of her education.
- Is she telling the truth about herself in Act 3 scene 2 lines 149–175? Explain your answer.
- She has spent all her young life on a country estate at Belmont, far from Venice. Suddenly she goes into court, with the reputation of a learned lawyer, before the Duke and the 'magnificoes'. She is the focus of all eyes, and a life hangs in the balance. What does this tell us about her?
- Portia is successful in rescuing Antonio from what looked like certain death. Does she have to continue and accuse Shylock of attempted murder? Do you think this accusation is planned, or a sudden idea? (Look at the language used in Act 4 scene 1 lines 348–356) The Duke and Antonio grant a small measure of mercy. What seems to be Portia's attitude? What do you think of her line, '*Art thou contented Jew? What dost thou say?*'

Bassanio
- Bassanio readily agrees to employ the fool, Launcelot. He dresses him in his own livery, with money he has borrowed, and takes him to Belmont. What do we already know about Bassanio's own foolishness?
- Portia's father has done his best to ensure that her hand in marriage will be won by a man whose values are sound. It must not be someone who is after her great fortune.
- The very first thing Bassanio says about Portia is '*In Belmont is a lady richly left*'. But he wins her. How does Bassanio know, perhaps better than anybody else that '*The world is still deceived with ornament*'? How, in fact, has he won Portia?

Secret files

In any play the writer presents us with key moments in the lives of the characters and leaves us to work out the rest of their biographies for ourselves. It is interesting to ask questions about those parts of the characters' lives that the writer does not tell us about. For example: how does Antonio set about preparing his ships for their voyages? Is he a thoughtful employer? What are Gratiano's bachelor apartments like? How did Jessica meet Lorenzo?

1 Choose one of the main characters.

2 Make up a list of questions about that character that you would like to have answered.

3 Build up a complete 'secret file' about your chosen character. Start with his or her birth, family and childhood and add information up to the end of the play.

4 Use all the relevant information you can find in the play. You can make up as much as you like providing nothing contradicts the facts of the play and the behaviour of your character in it.

5 Include a section on the character's attitudes and ideas. Try to show the origins of any key relationships in the play.

6 If you wish, and if appropriate to the character, continue the character's existence beyond the time of the play. For example, you could report on Lorenzo and the success, or otherwise, of his marriage to Jessica.

Quotables

When you are talking or writing about a character it is important to be able to back up your ideas by referring to the play: 'This is true because in Act 1 scene 2 she says this or does that.' You should have plenty of this kind of information for the main characters in your CHARACTER LOGS. You will need to keep some character information in your head and a good way of doing this is to search for 'the ideal quotation' for each character – the one line that absolutely sums up him or her. For example, Portia says of herself, '*I never did repent for doing good, Nor shall not now.*'

1 For each of the main characters find at least two short quotations. These may be something the character says or something another character says about them.

2 Select the best quotation from your list for each character.

3 Working in a group, try your quotations out on the others. Make a group list of the best quotation for each character.

Comparisons

When you first look at the list of characters for *The Merchant of Venice*, and even on a first reading of the early scenes, it is easy to think that all the young men are much the same. They are in the same social set. They all live in the bustling, gossipy marketplace that is Venice. They obviously spend a lot of time together.

It is not worth investigating Solanio and Salerio for differences, but for the other three: Bassanio, Lorenzo and Gratiano it is helpful to compare and contrast them.

Use four columns. The first should be the widest and the other three should have enough space for a tick or cross or a question mark.

- The first column should have the heading 'Comparisons' and the other three 'Bassanio', 'Lorenzo' and 'Gratiano' (see below).
- Continue the list of characteristics, considering Bassanio first and check whether the other two men share these features. Then do the same for the other two men.
- Use a question mark either for information you are simply not given in the play, or where you suspect a different truth from the one apparently given. For example: Does Gratiano marry for love, or might he think that Nerissa is so close to Portia that she will be well looked after financially?

Comparisons	Bassanio	Lorenzo	Gratiano
Young	✓	✓	✓
Idle	✓	✓	✓
Talkative	✓	✗	✓
Wastes money	✓	✓	?

Writing activities

Writing about the play

Much of the writing you have been asked to do on the
ACTIVITIES pages of this book has been personal or imaginative:
telling the reader about your own response to an aspect of the
play, or imagining that you were one of the characters in it.

You will also be asked to write about the play in a more formal
way, for example: 'The play could easily turn into a tragedy. How
are we made to feel that it will end happily?'

At first this kind of writing may seem rather daunting. It can
certainly be difficult to prepare for and organize. The notes on
these two pages are designed to help.

The question

What you must remember – first, last and all the time – is that
you have been asked a particular question. You have not been
asked to 'write all you know about *The Merchant of Venice*'. So
at all stages of your work you must focus on the question. And
there are two key questions you should ask yourself about it:
1 Am I sure that I understand what it means?
2 What is the best way to go about answering it?

Information and ideas

Before you can plan your writing in any detail, there are two
things you need to do:

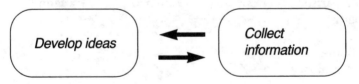

Each of these helps the other. Build up ideas by:
• talking to other people
• jotting down lists
• making a web diagram.

As you do so, you will begin to think of the information that you need. It is important to be able to back up each point you want to make by referring to something in the play – an action or a speech. You can use your SCENE and CHARACTER LOGS to help here. As you look at the logs and at the play itself you will begin to develop new ideas.

Making a plan

Some people can write well without making a plan, but this kind of more formal writing is difficult to do well without any plan at all. This is one way of planning:

1 Make a list of the main points you want to make.
2 Think of the best order to arrange these in. Remember that someone is going to read what you write; you need to keep their interest, so don't, for example, use up all your good ideas at the beginning so that the second half of your writing is boring. Try to make sure that one point leads naturally to the next.
3 Your last paragraph should state clearly your answer to the question – which you should have proved by everything else you have written.
4 Your first paragraph should introduce the topic – but don't give the game away at the very beginning!

The right tone of voice

If you are used to writing in personal and imaginative ways, you may find it difficult to achieve the right tone of voice for this kind of writing. As with other writing, it is important to think about the kind of person you are writing for. If it is an examination or test question, then you may well be writing for someone you have never met. So it may help you to imagine that your reader is a teacher from another school, someone who is not used to your way of writing and who does not know how you have been studying the play (and who does not necessarily share your sense of humour!).

Writing topics

Sometimes you may be asked to write a short response to a question or topic, while at other times you may be required to write at greater length. These two pages give practice in both.

Short answers

Each of these topics requires detailed attention to a particular act, scene or part of a scene. The section referred to is stated at the beginning of each one.

1 **Act 1 scene 1**

Now that you have read the play, do you find it easier to suggest reasons for Antonio's sadness?

2 **Act 1 scene 1**

By the end of Act 1 scene 1, you have met all Antonio's friends. Discuss his relationship with them.

3 **Act 1 scene 2**

Trace Portia's changes of mood in this scene and give reasons for them. What is Nerissa's influence?

4 **Act 1 scene 3**

We see several sides of Shylock in this scene. Decide what they are and use quotations to illustrate your answer.

5 **Act 2**

In this act Shylock is deserted by his servant and by his daughter. What do we learn about all three characters from these events?

6 **Act 2**

In the course of Act 2 we see the first two attempts to win Portia. Look at the way in which the two men make their decision and comment on the wisdom of Portia's father.

7 **Act 2 scene 6**

Jessica is Shylock's daughter, and a Jewess. Why don't the Venetians treat her as they treat her father?

8 **Act 3 scene 1**

Can you account for the fact that it is in Act 3 scene 1 that Shylock mentions 'revenge' for the first time? Look at what has happened to him and decide whether he changes in the course of Act 3 as a result.

9 **Act 3 scene 2**
You may have thought at first that Bassanio was mainly after Portia's money. How does scene 2 affect this opinion?

10 **Act 3 scene 2**
What have you learnt about Elizabethan expectations of courtship and marriage from this scene?

11 **Act 4 scene 1**
'It never pays to take a dispute to court.' Discuss with reference to Act 4.

12 **Act 5**
What is Act 5 for? Discuss.

Long answers

1 Show how the themes of love, friendship, money and marriage overlap in this play.

2 'Launcelot is absolutely essential to the balance of this play.' Discuss.

3 Whether Portia is on stage or not, she is central to every important action in the play. Do you agree? Give your reasons.

4 Which is the better title *The Merchant of Venice* or 'The Moneylender of Venice'? Give your reasons.

5 'Shakespeare faced many difficulties in trying to make Bassanio an attractive hero.' Do you agree?

6 'The magnificent sailing ships of the sixteenth century are an unseen presence throughout *The Merchant of Venice.*' Investigate this statement. (See THE SETTING AND THE MOOD, page 222.)

7 'Money is power.' Discuss, with reference to *The Merchant of Venice*.

8 'It would suit Shylock to have Antonio dead, and he thinks he's found a legal way to murder him.' Is this how you see the story?

9 'There are two Shylocks in *The Merchant of Venice* – the ogre and the human being.' Discuss.

10 'Is Shylock just a helpless victim or has he contributed to his own destruction?' Discuss.

Glossary

Alliteration: A figure of speech in which a number of words close to each other in a piece of writing begin with the same sound:

'Which touching but my gentle vessel's side
Would scatter all her spices on the stream,
Enrobe the roaring waters with my silks'

Alliteration helps to draw attention to these words.

Antithesis: A figure of speech in which the writer brings two opposite or contrasting ideas up against each other:

'There may as well be amity and life
'Twixt snow and fire, as treason and my love.'

Apostrophe: A figure of speech in which a character speaks directly to a person who is not present or to a personification (see below):

'Conscience', say I, 'you counsel well.' 'Fiend', say I, 'you counsel well.'

Aside: A speech which can be quite long, as in Act 1 scene 3 lines 38–49, or as short as a single remark, made by one of the characters for the ears of the audience alone, or purely for the benefit of another, named, character. The convention is that no-one else on the stage can hear it. Some critics suggest that this long aside of Shylock's should more accurately be called a *soliloquy* (see below).

Blank verse: See page 212

Caesura: From the Latin word meaning 'to cut'. This term is used for a pause or interruption in the middle of a line of verse.

'The moon shines bright. In such a night as this,
When the sweet wind did gently kiss the trees'

Dramatic irony: A situation in a play when the audience (and possibly some of the characters) know something one or more of the characters don't. In a pantomime, for example, young children will often shout to tell the hero that a dreadful monster is creeping up behind him, unseen. An example from *The Merchant of Venice* is the situation in the trial scene where only Portia, Nerissa and the audience know that Portia is Bassanio's wife, a woman and not a lawyer. This leads to lines which only the audience and Nerissa can appreciate, when Bassanio says he would sacrifice his wife for Antonio's life, and Portia says:

'Your wife would give you little thanks for that
If she were by to hear you make the offer.'

The same situation carries over, of course, into Act 5 and leads to the comic threats that the women will sleep with the 'men' who were given their rings.

Exeunt: A Latin word meaning 'They go away', used for the departure of characters from a scene.

Exit: A Latin word meaning 'He (or she) goes away', used for the departure of a character from a scene.

Hyperbole: Deliberate exaggeration, for dramatic effect. For example, when Bassanio realizes what misfortune he has brought on Antonio he says:

'Here is a letter lady;
The paper as the body of my friend,
And every word in it a gaping wound
Issuing life-blood.'

Irony: When someone says one thing and means another. Sometimes it is used to tease or satirize someone or, as here, it can express great bitterness. It should also make Antonio feel ashamed, but it doesn't. Shylock says to Antonio:

''Fair sir, you spat on me on Wednesday last,
You spurned me such a day, another time
*You called me dog; and for these **courtesies***
I'll lend you thus much moneys'?'

See also ***Dramatic irony***

Metaphor: A figure of speech in which one person, or thing, or idea is described as if it were another. Antonio has called Shylock a dog in the past. Now that Shylock has the upper hand he says:

'But since I am a dog, beware my fangs'

because he intends to savage Antonio, as a dog might.

Onomatopoeia: Using words that are chosen because they mimic the sound of what is being described:
'*Enrobe the roaring waters with my silks*'
The word '*roaring*' makes the imagined wreck seem real. The waters '*devour*' the merchandise like wild animals, and you hear the sound they make.

Oxymoron: A figure of speech in which the writer combines two ideas which are opposites. This frequently has a startling or unusual effect:
'*O happy torment, when my torturer*
Doth teach me answers for deliverance.'

Personification: Referring to a thing or an idea as if it were a person:
'*How sweet the moonlight sleeps upon this bank.*'

Play on words: see *Pun*

Pun: A figure of speech in which the writer uses a word that has more than one meaning. Both meanings of the word are used to make a joke. In the trial scene Antonio makes what he believes is his farewell speech. He assumes that Shylock will cut so close to his heart that he will kill him. He says he does not regret paying Bassanio's debt:
'*For if the Jew do cut but deep enough,*
I'll pay it presently with all my heart.'
meaning both 'willingly' and literally.
Sometimes the words are used twice. Here they suggest a similar though not identical sound, and a different meaning. Gratiano, jubilant at his and Bassanio's success at Belmont, says to Salerio:
'*We are the Jasons, we have won the fleece.*'
Salerio replies:
'*I would you had won the fleece that he hath lost.*' in a reference to Antonio's 'fleets' lost at sea.

Rhetorical question: A question used for effect, usually in argument or debate, sometimes in a soliloquy (see below). An answer is not expected. It would break the flow of the speech if it were offered. Shylock asks:
'*What should I say to you? Should I not say*

'*Hath a dog money? Is it possible*
A cur can lend three thousand ducats?''

The speaker may find it convenient to answer the question himself. The Prince of Morocco asks:

'*Or shall I think in silver she's immured,*
Being ten times undervalued to tried gold?
O sinful thought, never so rich a gem
Was set in worse than gold.'

Simile: A comparison between two things which the writer makes clear by using words such as 'like' or 'as':

'*The quality of mercy is not strained,*
It droppeth as the gentle rain from heaven'
'*An evil soul producing holy witness*
Is like a villain with a smiling cheek,
A goodly apple rotten at the heart.'

Soliloquy: When a character is alone on stage, or separated from the other characters in some way and speaks apparently to himself or herself. Launcelot is the only character in *The Merchant of Venice* who actually speaks alone on the stage, at the beginning of Act 2 scene 2. As we have seen (see *Aside*) some of Shylock's asides are referred to as soliloquies, and the three suitors' agonizings over their choice of casket have the effect of a soliloquy since they are not talking to anybody but themselves.